BrightRED Study Guide

CfE ADVANCED Higher

GEOGRAPHY

Phil Duffy

First published in 2017 by:
Bright Red Publishing Ltd
1 Torphichen Street
Edinburgh
EH3 8HX

A CIP record for this book is available from the British Library.

ISBN 978-1-349483-09-4

With thanks to:
PDQ Digital Media Solutions Ltd, Bungay (layout) and Dr Anne Horscroft (copy-edit).

Cover design and series book design by Caleb Rutherford – e i d e t i c.

Acknowledgements
Every effort has been made to seek all copyright-holders. If any have been overlooked, then Bright Red Publishing will be delighted to make the necessary arrangements.

Permission has been sought from all relevant copyright holders and Bright Red Publishing are grateful for the use of the following:

Images licensed by Ingram Image on pages 6, 8, 13, 17, 27, 38, 73, 75, 80, 85, 86, 88, 90, 93; Field Studies Council (CC BY 4.0)[1] (p 10); Dsdugan (Public Domain) (p 12); Gary Peeples/USFWS (CC BY 2.0)[2] (p 14); Joaquim Alves Gaspar (CC BY-SA 3.0)[3] (p 14); Wayne National Forest (CC BY 2.0)[2] (p 16); Douglas W. Jones (Public Domain) (p 16); Soil Science (CC BY 2.0)[2] (p 19); Three images © Anne Vaughan/Royal Alexandra and Albert School (pp 20, 21 & 79); SonoranDesertNPS (CC BY 2.0)[2] (pp 22 & 58); Geoff Morgan (p 23); Marcin Wichary (Public Domain) (p 28); Christiane Birr (CC BY-SA 2.0)[4] (p 28); Wellcome Images (CC BY 4.0)[1] (p 44); National Library of France (Public Domain) (p 46); NPS photo by Emily Brouwer (CC BY 2.0)[2] (p 53); geographypods.com/Public Domain (p 56); Koika (CC BY-SA 3.0)[3] (p 68); Blaser2 (CC BY-SA 3.0)[3] (p 70); NOAA/National Weather Service – National Centers for Environmental Prediction – Climate Prediction Center (Public Domain) (p 74); Ordnance Survey Map © Crown Copyright. All rights reserved. Licence number 100049324 (p 78); Mariusz Niedzwiedzki/Shutterstock.com (p 82); Robert Kropf (CC BY-SA 3.0 DE)[5] (p 93); Exam questions and answers © Scottish Qualifications Authority (pp 90 & 91).

[1] (CC BY 4.0) https://creativecommons.org/licenses/by/4.0/
[2] (CC BY 2.0) https://creativecommons.org/licenses/by/2.0/
[3] (CC BY-SA 3.0) https://creativecommons.org/licenses/by-sa/3.0/
[4] (CC BY-SA 2.0) https://creativecommons.org/licenses/by-sa/2.0/
[5] (CC BY-SA 3.0 DE) https://creativecommons.org/licenses/by-sa/3.0/de/

Printed and bound in the UK.

INTRODUCTION

DATA-GATHERING TECHNIQUES

DATA-PROCESSING TECHNIQUES

COURSE ASSESSMENT

INDEX

INTRODUCTION

COURSE SUMMARY

This is a revision guide and will help to supplement your course notes from school/college for the CfE Advanced Higher Geography course. If you studied CfE Higher Geography last year, you will be familiar with a range of geographical skills. This year, you will further develop your existing geographical skills and learn a wide range of new skills by undertaking practical activities.

COURSE OVERVIEW

CfE Advanced Higher Geography has the following course structure:

Geographical skills

In this section of the course, you will be required to provide evidence of your ability to:

- develop independent geographical research skills
- apply a wide range of research methods and fieldwork techniques
- apply a wide range of statistical, graphical and mapping techniques in an appropriate geographical context.

This section will help you to develop the wide range of skills required to successfully complete the coursework project folio: geographical study.

Geographical issues

In this section of the course, you will be required to provide evidence of your ability to:

'Critically evaluate viewpoints using evidence from a wide range of sources relating to a complex, current, geographical issue.'

This section will develop the wide range of skills required to successfully complete the coursework project folio: geographical issue.

COURSEWORK

DON'T FORGET 

The more organised you are, the better your project folio is likely to be.

The project folio is undertaken throughout the course and built up over time to be completed by the SQA submission date, which is usually in May. The project folio gives you an opportunity to develop your knowledge and understanding of geography at Advanced Higher level and to apply this knowledge and understanding to a study and issue of interest to you. You are free to research any appropriate study and issue of your own choice. For more details, refer to pp. 82–89 of this study guide.

Project folio
The project folio has 100 marks, two-thirds of the overall course mark. The total mark will be distributed as follows:

Section A: geographical study – 60 marks	Section B: geographical issue – 40 marks
Allows you to demonstrate the ability to undertake detailed research of a geographical nature which uses primary and/or secondary sources, to gather and process data and report findings appropriately. In order to complete section A (geographical study), you will: • justify the choice of a complex geographical topic to research • plan and carry out detailed research, which could include fieldwork • evaluate the research techniques and the reliability of data gathered • demonstrate a detailed knowledge and understanding of the topic being studied from wider reading • use a wide range of appropriate techniques to process the gathered information • analyse all the information that has been gathered, and processed, to identify and explain relationships • reach reasoned conclusion(s) supported by a wide range of evidence.	Allows you to demonstrate the ability to carry out a critical evaluation of a complex geographical issue by identifying viewpoints, from a wide range of sources, relating to the issue, and evaluating these viewpoints in a way that allows valid conclusions to be drawn. In order to complete section B (geographical issue), you will: • justify the choice of a current complex geographical issue to critically evaluate • undertake wider background reading from a wide range of sources relating to the geographical issue • summarise a wide range of viewpoints on the complex geographical issue • critically evaluate each of the viewpoints • reach reasoned conclusion(s) supported by a wide range of evidence.

Source: SQA Advanced Higher Geography Course Specification.

QUESTION PAPER – 50 MARKS

The exam lasts for 2 hours and 30 minutes and is made up of three sections, as outlined in the table. Questions will sample from across the course content – that is, skills, knowledge and understanding (for more details, see pp. 90–95.)

QUESTION NUMBER	GEOGRAPHICAL SKILL	NUMBER OF QUESTIONS TO BE ATTEMPTED	MARKS ALLOCATED (50 MARKS TOTAL)
1	**Map interpretation:** Extended-response questions of 2–6 marks. Using a 1:25 000-scale Ordnance Survey (OS) map and other supplementary items (for more details, see pp. 92 and 93)	Attempt all questions	20 marks
2	**Data-gathering and processing techniques:** Extended-response questions of 2–6 marks Questions may use supplementary items supplied with the question paper (for more details, see pp. 94 and 95)	Attempt all questions	10 marks
3	**Geographical data-handling:** Extended-response questions of 2–6 marks Questions will assess the interpretation and analysis of a given set of data, including statistical data, to evaluate the techniques used and their effectiveness in explaining geographical relations (for more details, see pp. 94 and 95)	Attempt all questions	20 marks

HOW THIS GUIDE CAN HELP YOU

There is no shortcut to passing any course at Advanced Higher level. To obtain a good pass requires consistent and regular revision over the duration of the course. The aim of this study guide is to help you to achieve success by providing you with concise and engaging coverage of the CfE Advanced Higher Geography course material. We recommend that you use this study guide in conjunction with your class notes to revise each skill area, to prepare for assessments, to prepare your submission of the project folio (study and issue) and to prepare for the final examination.

As you work through the pages of this study guide, think about the potential for links within and between the various geographical techniques:

- data-gathering techniques in physical geography (pp. 8–23)
- data-gathering techniques in human geography (pp. 24–37)
- statistical techniques (pp. 38–53)
- graphical techniques (pp. 54–63)
- mapping techniques (pp. 64–81)
- coursework (geographical study and geographical issue) (pp. 82–89)
- the question paper (pp. 90–95).

To respond to questions in the exam, you are expected to fully use the supplied supplementary items and your atlas to extract as much detail as possible to allow you to respond by writing well-developed answers within the context of the question.

You need to practise doing questions under timed conditions. The last thing you want is to run out of time in the examination.

Remember you can use an atlas in the examination.

GENERAL ADVICE AND SUPPORT

This study guide has been designed to ensure that you fulfil the requirements of the Advanced Higher Geography course. The guide is packed with useful advice, examples of all the Advanced Higher techniques, including web links to online videos, practical activities and academic articles to assist you to:

- develop a wide range of investigation skills while undertaking independent research, such as identifying appropriate research topics
- plan and manage a complex programme of research
- source, collect and record appropriate and reliable primary and secondary information
- develop methods of independent fieldwork
- present findings using appropriate conventions
- evaluate research methodology.

INDEPENDENT LEARNER

'Independent learning is a process, a method and a philosophy of education whereby a learner acquires knowledge by his or her own efforts and develops the ability for enquiry and critical evaluation.' (Forster 1972)

In practice, most learning involves independent elements such as:

- finding and collecting information
- making decisions about what to study and when
- carrying out investigations or projects
- learners learning at their own pace using ICT
- completing homework, extension work and coursework assignments.

This does not mean you do everything by yourself. Your centre (school/college) has a responsibility to provide support and assistance, but your teacher/lecturer should be seen less as an imparter of knowledge and more as a facilitator of learning – that is, don't expect your teacher/lecturer to tell you what to do or to do it for you.

However, you can expect reasonable assistance to allow you to progress through the course. The term 'reasonable assistance' is used to try to balance the need for support with the need to avoid giving too much assistance.

Much of the course will be undertaken on your own without direct supervision, producing your own work, but there should be opportunities for you to meet with your teacher/lecturer through:

- regular checkpoint/ progress meetings
- short spot-check personal interviews
- checklists to record your activity/progress.

Be prepared for meetings, having points to discuss and questions to ask, and be willing to accept advice. This is the sign of a good independent learner.

For your own personal safety, always tell someone where you are going and what you will be doing. Use your mobile phone to keep in contact.

WIDER READING

'No matter how busy you may think you are, you must find time for reading, or surrender yourself to self-chosen ignorance.' (Confucius)

A key difference between Higher and Advanced Higher study is the importance of wider reading. To achieve high grades, you need to read beyond the confines of selected textbooks and class notes. Although wider reading is essential, be aware that not every source – book, periodical, article or website – provides reliable and credible information. Always ensure you read a wide range of sources on a topic or issue.

ONLINE

Check out the meaning of the terms in the Glossary for this study guide at www.brightredbooks.net

RESEARCH/FIELDWORK NOTEBOOK

It is your responsibility, as an independent learner, to ensure the authenticity of your work – that is, it is all your own work.

You can work with others (e.g. fieldwork such as a beach-profile analysis), but you have to ensure you take part in all aspects of the activity. For example, you should change roles during the activity and not just be the person who records the results.

Keep a log/record of everything you do. This can be in a written notebook or on an electronic device. Write a plan for all activities, especially any fieldwork, taking into account your personal safety, all the equipment you require and whether you need the assistance of others to carry out a technique (e.g. stream analysis).

Record the date, time and location of any activity. Include detailed notes of the task/activity – for example:

- library research – sources used (titles, authors, page references) for later use when including references and bibliographies in your work
- fieldwork – location, activities, record of results – this will allow you to access secondary data relevant to that specific date and time (e.g. weather/river discharge/tides).

For each attempted activity, bullet-point a brief evaluation, such as:

- positive aspects – what went well
- negative aspects – what challenges/difficulties you experienced
- what you would do better next time
- next steps – including what you need to do to overcome the identified challenges/difficulties.

Your notebook can be used at regular meetings with your teacher/lecturer to show your progress, for discussion points about your research, to allow you to outline your next steps, and to seek advice and guidance.

Use your mobile phone and tablet to access relevant information.

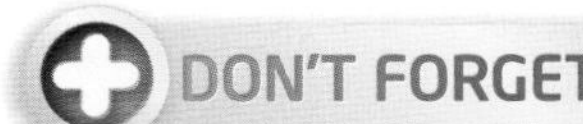

Check the SQA website to ensure you are using the latest version of any documentation.

SQA WEBSITES

The SQA provides a wealth of information to support you through the Advanced Higher Geography course across the following web pages:

- Advanced Higher Geography subject page
- SQA Understanding Standards
- SQA Secure.

You are strongly advised to use all available resources as part of your wider reading; as sources for research purposes; as guidance on how to be successful; and so that you are fully aware of the nature of and marking instructions for all assessments.

ONLINE

Find the links to the SQA pages mentioned here at www.brightredbooks.net

Always back up any materials, especially those collected on your phone/tablet, on a session-by-session basis.

USING TECHNOLOGY

Use technology to assist you throughout the course. You will be asked, at times, to carry out activities by hand, but even here you can use some technology – for example, do use a calculator for statistical calculations. There is scope within the Advanced Higher Geography course to use a wide range of technical hardware and software. As long as these are used appropriately, and with skill, to produce your own authenticated work, then take full advantage of what is available.

As an example, you could use a mobile phone/tablet not only for personal security, but also to:

- take images and to record findings and memos during fieldwork
- access guidance documentation on site during fieldwork
- look at maps and satellite images
- scan images of documentation for reference purposes that are not easily available elsewhere (e.g. at a library).

Keep your devices fully charged.

Knowledge is power: it enhances your ability to achieve.

INTRODUCTION

GENERAL ADVICE ON THE USE OF DATA-GATHERING TECHNIQUES

VIDEO LINK 

Watch the clips on the relevance of fieldwork in geography at www.brightredbooks.net

PURPOSE

It is important that you experience a wide range of research and fieldwork opportunities as part of your learning. Research involves the gathering of both primary and secondary data. Researching the 'how to ...' of a data-gathering technique is as important as actually carrying out that technique. Learning by doing extends your knowledge and understanding of a data-gathering technique. This does not mean, however, that you have to carry out fieldwork for all the data-gathering techniques listed in the table.

Learning how to carry out research and gather data in a relevant way is a core feature of the Advanced Higher Geography course and leads to a greater appreciation of the key core skills at this level, such as wider reading and the use of primary and secondary data collection. You are expected to know and understand the data-gathering techniques in the table for the examination. Within the context of the unit on geographical skills and the coursework (the geographical study and the geographical issue), you are free to use any appropriate and relevant data-gathering technique.

DATA-GATHERING TECHNIQUES: PHYSICAL GEOGRAPHY	DATA-GATHERING TECHNIQUES: HUMAN GEOGRAPHY
Beach-profile analysis	Environmental-quality survey
Microclimate analysis	Interview design and implementation
Pebble analysis	Pedestrian survey (pedestrian count)
Slope analysis	Perception studies
Soil analysis	Questionnaire design and Implementation
Stream analysis	Rural land-use mapping
Vegetation analysis	Traffic survey (traffic count)
	Urban land-use mapping

Candidates who use appropriate and relevant data-gathering techniques within the context of their coursework are more likely to achieve higher marks. It is not about the number of data-gathering techniques you include, but their relevance and sophistication – for example, the collection of relevant data to identify relationships, or differences, that will also allow more detailed analyses.

The techniques listed in the table are explained on pp. 10–37 under specific headings to give you the information required to carry out a technique and to answer the related examination questions, including how you can process the collected data.

The links to videos and online materials in this guide are for illustrative purposes and will help to support your learning. You are free to use other similar resources that you might identify during your research.

ONLINE 

Check out ideas and suggestions for research and the Glossary at www.brightredbooks.net

PLANNING YOUR RESEARCH AND FIELDWORK

Plan the purpose of your research to get the most out of the experience. This includes both library- and field-based research. The latter involves more challenges, but the following advice applies to both areas of work.

- Be clear about your aim and what you are trying to prove. A 'hypothesis' or 'null hypothesis' can be developed from your aim/research questions. For example, your hypothesis might be 'there **is a** significant relationship between stream velocity and distance downstream', and your null hypothesis might be 'there **is no** significant relationship between stream velocity and distance downstream'.
- Choose a location for your research, or fieldwork, that allows you to gather the right kind of data. Be aware of potential challenges or risks, such as working in a river.
- Seek permission from the landowner before carrying out fieldwork – for example, you need to seek permission from the owner/management company before carrying out a questionnaire in a shopping centre.
- Make a pre-visit check of the fieldwork location and its suitability for your research.
- Consider how you and your equipment will get to the fieldwork location.
- Equipment can be either generic or specific.

What equipment will I need?

Generic items (equipment needed for all techniques):

- a research/fieldwork notebook
- a mobile phone/tablet
- an OS map extract of the chosen area or similar
- waterproof clothing as appropriate, such as wellingtons/waders
- data-collection sheets
- a clipboard
- pencils
- a camera
- plastic bags to collect samples or protect your data sheets.

See pp. 10–37 for examples of the specialist equipment needed for particular techniques.

SAMPLING METHODS

Sampling is a process used in fieldwork in which a pre-determined number of observations are taken from a larger population. The sampling method used will depend on the type of research to be undertaken. This study guide focuses on three simple sampling methods: random, stratified and regular/systematic sampling.

THINGS TO DO AND THINK ABOUT

As you work through the data-gathering techniques in this unit, think about the links that exist within these techniques and between the other geographical techniques in this study guide:

- data-gathering techniques for physical geography (pp. 8–23)
- data-gathering techniques for human geography (pp. 24–37)
- statistical techniques (pp. 38–53)
- graphical techniques (pp. 54–63)
- mapping techniques (pp. 64–81)
- coursework (the geographical study and geographical issue) (pp. 82–89)
- the question paper (pp. 90–95).

ONLINE

Check out the links at www.brightredbooks.net for more details on planning fieldwork.

ONLINE

Use the calculator at www.brightredbooks.net to determine the sample size required, such as how many people you need to interview to obtain results that reflect the target population. The calculator will also allow you to determine the level of precision in an existing sample.

ONLINE

Check out the links to websites at www.brightredbooks.net for more information on sampling methods.

VIDEO LINK

Check out the videos on sampling techniques at www.brightredbooks.net

DON'T FORGET

Decide your sampling strategy before gathering any data.

ONLINE

Check out the examples of mind-maps used to plan research and fieldwork at www.brightredbooks.net

BEACH-PROFILE ANALYSIS

PURPOSE

To measure the transverse profile (shape and morphology) of a beach from a fixed point set up behind the beach down to the low water mark. Profiles taken at different times and locations can be compared to illustrate and quantify changes in beach width, height, volume and shape. They can also be used to show the relationships between the beach profile and other factors – for example, the rock type, cliff profile and sediment size or shape.

DON'T FORGET

Refer to the generic equipment list on pp. 8 and 9.

EQUIPMENT

The specific equipment needed to complete a beach-profile analysis includes:

- a tape measure
- an Abney level and clinometer or pantometer
- ranging poles
- a compass
- a recording sheet.

VIDEO LINK

Check out the clips at www.brightredbooks.net to learn more about beach profiling and using an Abney level.

ONLINE

Check out the links at www.brightredbooks.net to learn more about planning and carrying out fieldwork.

VIDEO LINK

Head to the Digital Zone to watch a video on how to use a clinometer.

ONLINE

To find out how to make a pantometer, head to www.brightredbooks.net

VIDEO LINK

Check out the clip at www.brightredbooks.net to learn more about how to draw a beach profile.

METHODOLOGY

Refer to both the generic advice on pp. 8 and 9 and the following specific points.

This technique is, by its nature, a group activity. You must ensure that you are involved in all aspects of the technique to be able to claim that the research is your work shared with others.

First, you need to set up your profile locations.

Using a clinometer and ranging poles to measure the angle of a beach profile.

- Decide an appropriate sampling strategy using the guidance on p. 9.
- Locate sampling points along the beach by visually noting the main changes in slope angle along the profile, and use these as the basis for sections within the profile (e.g. A–B, B–C, C–D in the diagram). You can sketch a rough profile to indicate the break of slope points.
- At each sample point, identify and stake the reference point (H) using a ranging pole. Take a photo to record the position of this point for future reference.
- Use your compass to work out the bearing/orientation of the profile line. This will be perpendicular to the beach face. Place a ranging pole at the end of the profile line (A). Point A should ideally be the low tide mark (0 m), or as close to this as is safe. Maintain the bearing as you progress along the profile.
- For each section, use the Abney level and clinometer to take a bearing. Read and record the slope angle (ii) between points. The bearing must be taken at a point on the ranging pole at point A that coincides with the eye level of the person using the Abney level and clinometer. You must aim the Abney level and clinometer at the same level on the ranging pole at point B. Use the stripes on the ranging poles to help.
- Measure the ground distance of the section (O), and record this information with the slope angle.
- Repeat this process for each identified break in slope.
- If appropriate for your research, write down as many comments and observations as possible (e.g. grain size, bedform, debris lines or berm crest).

Pantometers can be used by one person, and the slope can be surveyed systematically at short, regular intervals.

contd

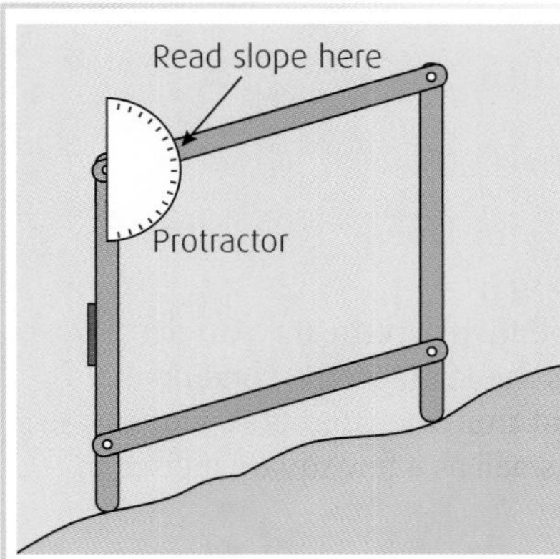

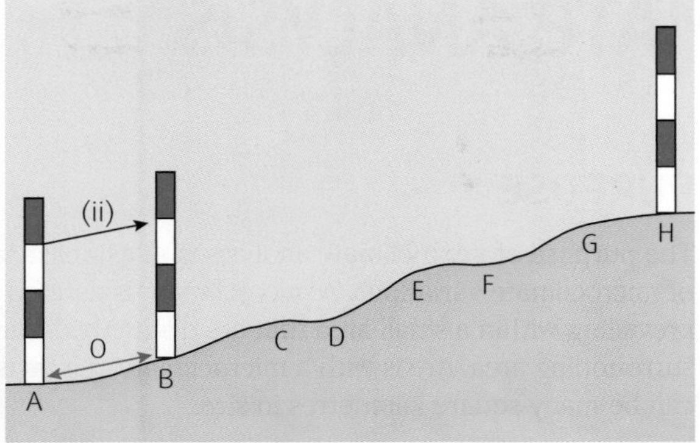

Surveying the morphology of a beach using a pantometer and ranging poles.

Data collected by either method can be used to create a beach profile.

BEACH-PROFILE DATA SHEET

Site Name: Irvine Beach Profile 3

Date: 18/12/17 Surveyors: M Smith & J Smart

Observations: e.g. Lots of debris on the beach washed up from last week's storm

Measurement down from the top of the reference mark: 1.01 metres

Beach segment	Length of segment (metres)	Slope angle (degrees & minutes)
A–B	5·73	−7° 00′
B–C	4·29	−4° 00′
C–D	1·25	+3° 00′
D–E	1·85	−1° 30′
E–F	6·98	−8° 00′
F–G		
G–H		
H–I		

Example of a beach-profile analysis data record sheet.

DON'T FORGET

Computer software may assist you in analysing your collected data – for example, the *X-Y* scatterplot in Excel or similar spreadsheets (*X* = distance, *Y* = angle between sections).

DON'T FORGET

Check you have sufficient data to process – if not, go gather more!

DON'T FORGET

Evaluate your research and consider whether the data collected is sufficient to meet the needs of your initial research questions. If not, you may need to carry out further field research.

CONSIDERATIONS AND LIMITATIONS

- Safety is a major consideration when carrying out fieldwork on a beach. Tides and the time you need or have to carry out fieldwork must be carefully checked and assessed. Working in groups to carry out several profiles along the beach at the same time and then sharing the results is an appropriate and efficient methodology.
- A balance needs to be struck between the time available and the need for a number of profiles across the width of the beach to ensure the validity of your results.
- To record accurate angle readings, the ranging poles need to be held straight and not allowed to sink into the sand.
- User error, or a lack of familiarity with using a clinometer, can produce invalid readings.
- The pantometer must be kept vertical when taking readings.

ONLINE TEST

Test yourself on beach profiles on our Digital Zone at www.brightredbooks.net

THINGS TO DO AND THINK ABOUT

Refer to the generic advice on pp. 8 and 9 and the following specific points.

Think about the possible links that beach-profile analysis may have with other geographical techniques in this study guide. For example:

- combining beach-profile analysis with pebble analysis, soil analysis and vegetation analysis to compare different sections of the same beach or sections of different beaches – for example, a sand beach compared with a pebble beach (pp. 10–23)
- combining beach-profile analysis, pebble analysis and vegetation analysis with environmental-quality survey and perception studies to carry out a beach-quality survey (pp. 24–37)
- statistical testing, such as mean pebble size or the Spearman rank correlation coefficient (pp. 38–53)
- graphical, such as bar or scatter graphs (pp. 54–63)
- mapping, such as annotations, cross-sections, transects and beach profiles (pp. 64–81.)

MICROCLIMATE ANALYSIS

PURPOSE

The purpose of microclimate analysis is to establish, and then explain, the pattern of microclimate variations. A microclimate is defined as the atmospheric conditions prevailing within a small area that are distinctly different from the conditions in the surrounding area. Areas with a microclimate can be as small as a few square metres or can be many square kilometres in size.

Geography and topography are the main causes of microclimates. For example, south-facing slopes in the northern hemisphere and north-facing slopes in the southern hemisphere are exposed to more direct sunlight than the opposite slopes and are therefore warmer for longer periods of time.

Effect of aspect on microclimates.

EQUIPMENT

Refer to the generic equipment list on pp. 8 and 9.

The weather instruments you use, the background theoretical information you require and the secondary data relevant to your microclimate analysis will vary according to the specific geographical location of the analysis.

The specific equipment needed to complete a microclimate analysis includes:

- weather instruments, such as a weather vane, an anemometer or ventimeter, a thermometer, a (whirling) hygrometer/psychrometer, a rain gauge and a barometer
- map(s) of the study area, a compass, chart of the Beaufort scale, a light meter, wind-chill information, data sheets, a guide to identify plant types/species and recording sheets.

METHODOLOGY

Refer to the generic advice on pp. 8 and 9 and the following specific points.

Make sure you understand and appreciate the geographical theory behind microclimates. Be clear on your aim and what you are trying to prove before you start to gather data. A hypothesis can be developed from your aim and research questions, such as 'there is a significant relationship between temperature and distance from the central business district of ...'.

The methodology is much the same whether you are measuring the microclimate in a woodland, grassland or urban area.

Obtain a large-scale map or plan of the study area (you might consider drawing your own map).

Decide your sampling strategy, including:

- the number and location of sites where data will be collected/stratified/sampled and/or the sample intervals along a transect (regular sampling) – for example, to determine whether temperature decreases on moving away from a city centre

contd

ONLINE 

When planning the scope of your microclimate analysis, read the UK Meteorological Office's fact sheet at www.brightredbooks.net

VIDEO LINK 

Check out the clips at www.brightredbooks.net to learn more about microclimates.

ONLINE 

Follow the links at www.brightredbooks.net for the latest weather forecast/information.

ONLINE  

Use secondary data sources – for example, data is available free from the UK Meteorological Office website at www.metoffice.gov.uk

ONLINE 

Check out the link at www.brightredbooks.net for some ideas and advice.

- the weather variables to be measured and recorded, such as the temperature, wind speed/direction and humidity
- the timing and frequency of readings – you may need to take measurements on a regular basis
- if appropriate to your study, the identification of plant types within a 1 m radius using a field guide.

Number each sampling location on your map and link this number to the corresponding data on the recording sheet. Repeat for each location.

Example:

To plan and carry out a microclimate analysis to find a suitable site for a new outdoor swimming pool.

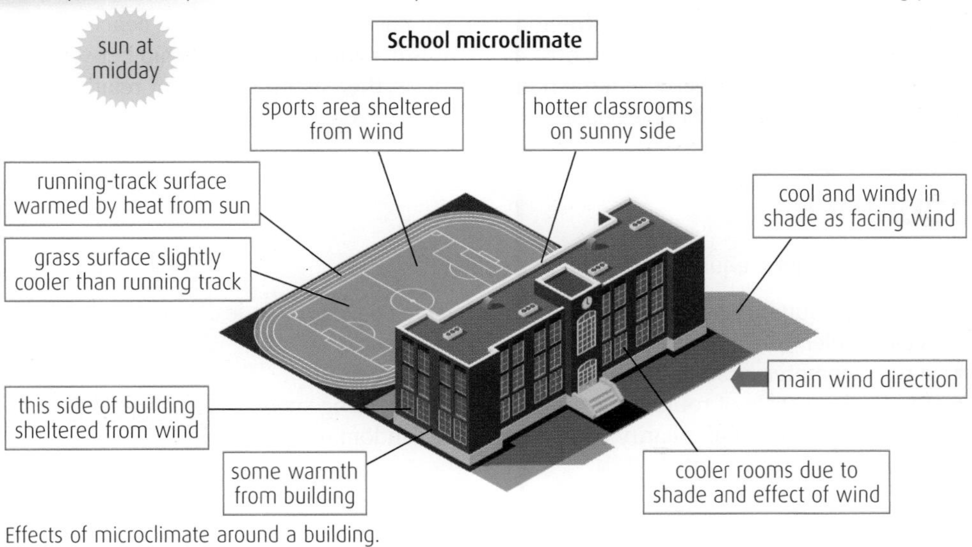

Effects of microclimate around a building.

DON'T FORGET

Taking several readings and finding the average can increase the validity of results.

DON'T FORGET

Review your data sheets to ensure they are complete.

DON'T FORGET

Always be methodical in what you do.

DON'T FORGET

Evaluate your research and consider whether the data collected is sufficient to meet the needs of your initial research questions. If not, you may have to carry out further field research.

CONSIDERATIONS AND LIMITATIONS

- To ensure sufficient reliable and valid data is collected for analysis, the sampling method has to be one that determines the locations to be sampled and the timing and frequency of recordings.
- Different weather instruments operate differently, and you need to be familiar with their operation to ensure that relevant and accurate data is collected.
- Digital instruments are more accurate and precise than analogue instruments, but only if fully powered and calibrated correctly.
- Consider the practicality of checking all gauges at the same time.
- The effects of vegetation and the interception of rain or buildings providing shelter should be noted, but may be interesting variables to investigate in their own right.

ONLINE TEST

Test yourself on microclimates on our Digital Zone at www.brightredbooks.net

THINGS TO DO AND THINK ABOUT

Refer to the generic advice on pp. 8 and 9 and the following specific points.

Think about the possible links that microclimate analysis may have with other geographical techniques in this study guide. For example:

- combining microclimate analysis with slope analysis, soil analysis, soil temperature and vegetation analysis to compare similar or contrasting areas within a woodland environment (pp. 10–23)
- combining microclimate analysis with an environmental-quality survey, perception studies or interviews – for example, to investigate the potential relationship between temperature and building height/layout (pp. 24–37)
- statistical testing, such as the Spearman rank correlation coefficient (pp. 38–53)
- graphical techniques, such as line graphs, bar graphs or pie charts positioned on a base map, or a scatter graph (pp. 54–63)
- mapping techniques, such as tracings and annotations, or a transect (pp. 64–81).

PEBBLE/SEDIMENT ANALYSIS

DON'T FORGET 

Read more about the hypothesis and null hypothesis on pages 38–39.

ONLINE 

Check out the websites at www.brightredbooks.net for more advice.

VIDEO LINK 

Watch the clip at www.brightredbooks.net for information on bedload sampling and analysis.

ONLINE 

For good advice and guidance on sediment size and coastal processes, follow the links at www.brightredbooks.net

VIDEO LINK 

Check out the clips at www.brightredbooks.net to learn more about pebble analysis.

Using a calliper to measure the three axes of a pebble.

PURPOSE

To measure the size, shape and fabric (orientation and disposition) of particles to learn about the processes involved in the erosion, transportation and deposition of material. This technique can be used to measure sediments on a beach, in a river bed, within glacial deposits and in weathered rock.

In this section, the focus is on the size and shape of particles in relation to a beach and river bed – for example, the hypothesis 'there **is a** significant relationship between pebble size and pebble shape' and the null hypothesis 'there **is no** significant relationship between pebble size and pebble shape'.

EQUIPMENT

Refer to the generic equipment list on pp. 8 and 9.

The specific equipment needed to complete a pebble analysis includes:

- a clear ruler
- a pebbleometer or stoneboard
- the Cailleux scale of roundness and/ or Power's scale of angularity
- a tape measure
- a quadrat
- a compass
- a recording sheet
- a random number table.

METHODOLOGY

Refer to the generic advice on pp. 8 and 9 and the following specific points.

For reasons of safety and practicality, this technique is best carried out as a group activity. You must ensure that you are involved in all aspects of the technique to be able to claim that the research is your work shared with others.

Decide an appropriate sampling strategy using the guidance on p. 9. Quadrats can be used to select sediments for sampling. Alternatively, ten surface pebbles touching your foot can be selected at each location.

Example:

Rivers: use the locations of depth readings across the channel as sample points for pebble/sediment analysis. Refer to the methodology outlined on pp. 20 and 21.

Coasts: use the sections along the beach-profile sample as sample points – refer to the methodology outlined on pp. 10 and 11 – or across the width of the beach (linking to the process of longshore drift).

The following procedures should be used at each sample point.

- Reach down with your index finger extended and select the first pebble it touches.
- Use the callipers, pebbleometer or stoneboard to measure the long (*a*), intermediate (*b*) and short (*c*) axes of the pebble. The three axes must be at right angles to each other. Average the length of the axes to give the mean particle size.

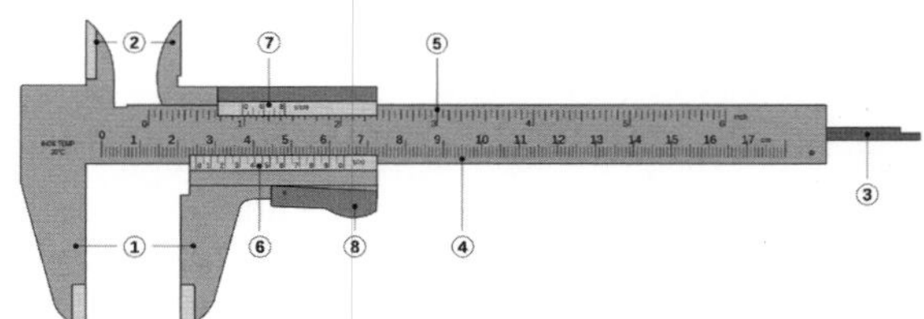

Callipers used for measuring pebble dimensions.

- Record the measurements on the recording sheet – see example.

contd

- If appropriate for your research, write down as many additional background comments and observations as possible (e.g. grain size, presence of bedforms, debris lines or berm crests).

Record the measurements onto the recording sheet.

Location..														Name(s)..			
Transect no..........................				Length..										Date/time..............................	Low tide................................		
Site no.	Distance from sea (m)	Slope angle		Sample size (cm)										Mean (a) axis	Mean m.p.s.	Range m.p.s.	Mean index of roundness
				1	2	3	4	5	6	7	8	9	10				
1	4	1·5°	(a)												Largest	Smallest	
			(b)														
			(c)														
			m.p.s.														
			1–6														
			r														
			R														

Example of a recording sheet. m.p.s. is the mean particle size.

- Repeat this process, perhaps ten times per location, ensuring that the distance from the bank or shore line is recorded.

Review the data sheets to ensure they are complete.

CONSIDERATIONS AND LIMITATIONS

- Deciding on the sampling strategy is very important in reducing subjectivity and increasing the validity of your results.
- To avoid bias, consideration needs to be given to the size of the sample and the method used to select the pebbles.
- The sample size should be large enough to provide a representative sample of the parent population, yet not too large to be unmanageable.
- The sharpest point of a stone is measured using the Cailleux scale of roundness; and judgement of this may vary from person to person, creating subjectivity.
- The use of visual charts such as Power's scale of angularity can also be subjective.
- In reality, using Power's scale will mostly give an angularity of class five or six.
- Anything that may affect the results should be noted – for example, recent storms or management structures that might have altered the composition of beach material.

A sampling method should always be adopted to avoid the temptation to select pebbles.

DON'T FORGET

Evaluate your research and consider whether the data collected is sufficient to meet the needs of your initial research questions. If not, you may have to carry out further field research.

THINGS TO DO AND THINK ABOUT

Refer to the generic advice on pp. 8 and 9 and the following specific points.

Think about the possible links that pebble analysis has with other geographical techniques in this study guide. For example:

- combining pebble analysis with beach-profile analysis, slope analysis, soil analysis or stream analysis to compare two different sections of the same beach/stream or similar sections of two different beaches/streams (pp. 10–23)
- combining beach-profile analysis, pebble analysis and vegetation analysis with environmental-quality surveys, perception studies or interviews to investigate the potential for the growth in tourism between a pebble beach and a sand beach (pp. 24–37)
- statistical testing such as mean pebble size or the Spearman rank correlation coefficient (pp. 38–53)
- the use of graphical techniques, such as bar charts and scatter graphs (pp. 54–63)
- the use of mapping techniques, such as annotations, cross sections, transects and beach profiles (pp. 64–81).

Test yourself on pebble analysis on our Digital Zone at www.brightredbooks.net

SLOPE ANALYSIS

VIDEO LINK 

Check out the video at www.brightredbooks.net on how to calculate the gradient of a slope.

PURPOSE

The purpose of slope analysis is to measure and produce a profile (shape/morphology) of a slope. The steepness, or gradient, of slopes is one of the main determinants of how land is used. In general, the steeper the slope, the less likely it is to be used economically – although leisure pursuits such as rock-climbing and skiing rely on steep slopes.

Slope transects can be used to draw profiles of river, coastal and glacial features, such as valleys, moraines, beaches, dunes and drumlins. They can also be used to show the gradients of rivers, roads or railway lines.

In measuring slopes, we can investigate the relationship between the angle, height and aspect of the slopes, the vegetation cover and type, the soil depth and moisture content, and the ways the land is used.

EQUIPMENT

Refer to the generic equipment list on pp. 8 and 9.

The specific equipment needed to complete a slope analysis includes:

- a tape measure
- ranging poles
- an Abney level and clinometer or pantometer
- a compass
- a levelling method – tripod, spirit level and plumb line
- a recording sheet – see example on pp. 10 and 11 (beach-profile analysis)
- an OS map showing the area of study.

Using a clinometer.

DON'T FORGET 

Find out about transects on pp. 80–81.

VIDEO LINK 

Check out the video on how to use an Abney level at www.brightredbooks.net

METHODOLOGY

Refer to the generic advice on pp. 8 and 9 and the following specific points.

This technique is, by its nature, a group activity. You must ensure that you are involved in all aspects of the technique to be able to claim that the research is your work shared with others.

Check out a similar methodology used on pp. 10 and 11 (beach-profile analysis).

The following method can be used to set up your profile locations.

- Use an appropriate sampling strategy using the guidance on p. 9.
- Decide on a line of transect across a field or area of land (pp. 80 and 81).
- Use a compass to work out the bearing/orientation of the transect line.
- Use an OS map to identify the height of the starting point.
- Take a photo to record the position of this point for future reference.
- Break the transect into sections using any identifiable breaks in the slope.
- Sketch a rough profile of the transect indicating the break-of-slope points.
- Label these break-of-slope points A, B, C and so on.
- For each section, use the Abney level and clinometer to take a bearing. Read and record the slope angle (ii) – for example, from point A to point B. The bearing must be taken at a point on the ranging pole at point A that coincides with the eye level of the person using the Abney level and clinometer. You must aim the Abney level and clinometer at the same level on the ranging pole at point B. Use the stripes on the ranging poles to assist with this process.
- Use the tape to measure and record the distance between A and B.

An Abney level.

contd

- Move the first pole to the end of the second section and repeat the process until the whole transect is covered.
- If appropriate for your research, write down as many comments and observations as possible (e.g. aspect, vegetation cover, soil depth, moisture content and land use).

CONSIDERATIONS AND LIMITATIONS

Refer to the 'considerations and limitations' section for beach-profile analysis and the following points.

- The recorded data from a slope analysis could be plotted onto a graph to show the overall change in slope height and the change for each section. The graph can then be annotated with any points of interest – for example, areas of the sections in which crops would not grow properly, evidence of erosion or different vegetation cover.
- You could use an OS map of the area under analysis to calculate/check the gradient of a slope.
- There are other methods that could be used to survey a slope, such as using a pantometer to step your way downhill or uphill along your line of transect.

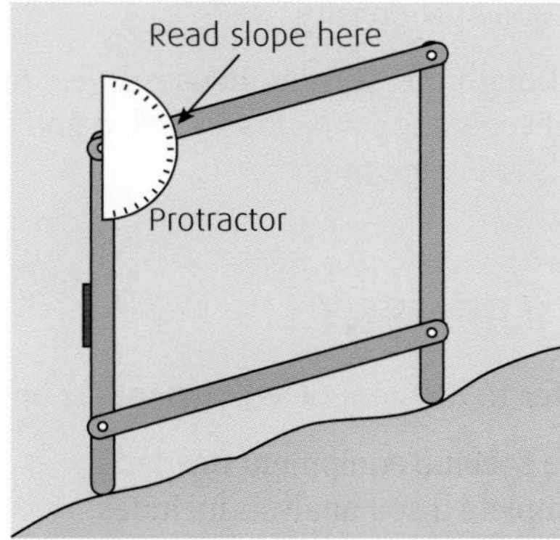

Using a pantometer.

Levelling, a traditional method of measuring a slope, gives you an immediate gradient, although you have to perform a further calculation to obtain the angle of the slope.

THINGS TO DO AND THINK ABOUT

Refer to the generic advice on pp. 8 and 9 and the following specific points.

Think about the possible links that slope analysis has with other geographical techniques in this study guide. For example:

- combining slope analysis with beach-profile analysis, soil analysis, pebble analysis or vegetation analysis to compare two different sections of the same slope/beach or similar sections of two different slopes/beaches (pp. 10–23)
- combining slope analysis and vegetation analysis with interviews, questionnaires and rural land-use mapping to investigate the environmental and ecological impact of modern farming practices (pp. 24–37)
- statistical testing such as Spearman rank correlation coefficient (pp. 38–53)
- using graphical techniques, such as line graphs (pp. 54–63)
- mapping techniques, such as field sketches, annotations, cross-sections and transects (pp. 64–81).

VIDEO LINK

Check out the video on how to proceed at www.brightredbooks.net

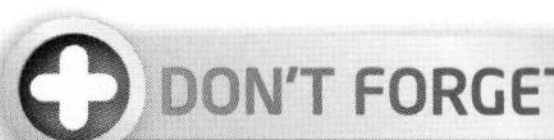

DON'T FORGET

Review the data sheets to ensure they are complete.

DON'T FORGET

Evaluate your research and consider whether the data collected is sufficient to meet the needs of your initial research questions. If not, you may have to carry out further field research.

VIDEO LINK

If you are interested in extending the scope of the slope analysis to look into the underlying geology, then check out the videos at www.brightredbooks.net

ONLINE TEST

Check these methods, recording sheets and further advice at www.brightredbooks.net

SOIL ANALYSIS

VIDEO LINK 

Check out the videos at wwww.brightredbooks.net for more information on soils, soil formation and soil profiles.

ONLINE 

Check out the websites at wwww.brightredbooks.net for some learning ideas and suggestions about soils.

PURPOSE

This technique is used to analyse the composition, texture and physical and chemical properties of soils. Geographers are interested not only in the characteristics of soils but also in how soil quality relates to the patterns of vegetation and agricultural potential.

Analysis of soils can include the following:

- soil sampling
- soil profiles
- soil temperature
- soil texture
- soil bulk density
- soil infiltration rates
- water content
- soil organic content
- soil chemistry (e.g. pH, nitrate levels).

Although this section focuses solely on soils, you should be aware that, in reality, soils and vegetation are closely linked and analyses often consider the relationship between soils and vegetation.

EQUIPMENT

Refer to the generic equipment list on pp. 8 and 9.

The specific equipment needed to complete a soil analysis includes:

- a trowel or spade
- a soil auger
- a pH probe and testing kit
- temperature and moisture probes
- soil infiltration equipment.

For a transect sample, you will need:

- ranging poles
- a tape measure
- a rope
- a compass
- record sheets.

METHODOLOGY

Refer to the generic advice on pp. 8 and 9 and the following specific points.

This technique has two distinct activities: (1) field research and (2) laboratory analysis.

This technique could be completed as a group activity. You must ensure that you are involved in all aspects of the technique to be able to claim that the research is your work shared with others.

Check out a similar methodology on pp. 10 and 11 (beach-profile analysis), pp. 11 and 12 (microclimate analysis), pp. 16 and 17 (slope analysis) and pp. 22 and 23 (vegetation analysis).

VIDEO LINK 

Check out the videos at www.brightredbooks.net for more information on soil sampling.

ONLINE 

Check out the website at www.brightredbooks.net about how to conduct soil analysis using sampling.

Soil sampling

The sampling method should be appropriate to gather sufficient samples to answer your research questions. Review the guidance on p. 9.

Location:

- if there is a gradient with a steady change in soil depth, or underlying geology, then use a systematic sampling along a transect (pp. 80 and 81) with samples collected at regular distances or altitudes (soil catena)
- if there is no gradient, random sampling is used (e.g. within an orchard or across a field)
- if you are comparing soils from two different areas, then collect sufficient samples to make any statistical test statistically significant (e.g. a minimum of ten samples).

contd

Depth of sampling:
- if you are looking at soil formation, then take samples from different depths in the soil profile
- if you are looking at the quality of soil along a transect, then collect samples from a consistent depth in the L–E horizons (see figure).

A transect is a line across a habitat or part of a habitat. It can be as simple as a string or rope placed in a line on the ground.

Check out how to set up a transect on pp. 11 and 12 (beach-profile analysis), pp. 16 and 17 (slope analysis) and pp. 22 and 23 (vegetation analysis).

The term 'soil catena' refers to the sequence of distinct soils located down a slope. Each soil type varies with relief and drainage, but all share the same climate and underlying parent material. These soil sequences can be found when following a transect from a hilltop to the valley bottom.

Field research:
While on location, there are a number of techniques you can use to collect data, including: soil sampling (soil profiles, soil temperature, soil texture and soil infiltration rates).

Soil horizons.

The horizons may be further subdivided. In this soil profile, the A horizon has been divided into four pedological horizons:
- (L) leaf litter
- (F) fermenting leaf litter
- (H) humus
- (E) eluvial

These lie above the (B) or illuvial horizon.

Laboratory analysis:

The collected samples should be analysed in the laboratory as soon as possible after fieldwork to identify the following attributes:
- water content
- soil organic content
- soil chemistry (e.g. pH, nitrate levels)
- soil texture (using a soil sieve and soil sedimentation)
- soil bulk density.

CONSIDERATIONS AND LIMITATIONS

Refer to the 'considerations and limitations' sections for beach-profile analysis, microclimate analysis, slope analysis and vegetation analysis, and the following points.

Soil analysis combines a range of techniques, including the use of sampling techniques, transects and laboratory experiments.

The recorded data from soil analysis can be plotted onto a graph showing the plant type, height change in each section. The graph can then be annotated with any points of interest – for example, the areas of the sections in which plants would not grow properly, evidence of erosion and different types of vegetation cover.

THINGS TO DO AND THINK ABOUT

Refer to the generic advice on pp. 8 and 9 and the following specific points.

Think about the possible links that soil analysis has with other geographical techniques in this study guide. For example:
- combining soil analysis with beach-profile analysis, microclimate analysis, pebble analysis, slope analysis and vegetation analysis to compare soil properties on a slope (pp. 10–23)
- combining slope analysis, soil analysis and vegetation analysis with interviews, questionnaires and rural land-use mapping to investigate the impact of afforestation/ deforestation in a rural area (pp. 24–37)
- statistical testing, such as the Spearman rank correlation coefficient (pp. 38–53)
- graphical techniques, such as triangular graphs and soil profiles (pp. 54–63)
- mapping techniques, such as annotations and transects (pp. 64–81).

VIDEO LINK

Watch the videos on how to set up a transect at www.brightredbooks.net

ONLINE

Check out www.brightredbooks.net to find out about the methods used to carry out fieldwork and laboratory techniques.

ONLINE

Check out the websites at www.brightredbooks.net for further considerations and limitations.

DON'T FORGET

Evaluate your research and consider whether the data collected is sufficient to meet the needs of your initial research questions. If not, you may have to carry out further field research.

ONLINE TEST

Test yourself on soil analysis on our Digital Zone at www.brightredbooks.net

STREAM ANALYSIS

PURPOSE

Stream analysis measures streams in terms of their size and shape, their flow velocities and discharge levels. This type of primary research provides ample opportunities for the gathering, processing and analysis of data to illustrate relationships between variables.

The Bradshaw model is a theoretical model that shows the expected changes in a stream as it flows downstream.

EQUIPMENT

Refer to the generic equipment list on pp. 8 and 9.

The specific equipment needed to complete a stream analysis includes:

- a tape measure (long and waterproof) (can also be used for cross-section)
- a metre rule (ranging poles can also be used)
- a flow meter (hydro-prop) or vane or a floating object (e.g. an orange)
- a stop-watch.

METHODOLOGY

Refer to the generic advice on pp. 8 and 9 and the following specific points.

Planning

For reasons of safety and practicality, this technique is best done as a group activity. You must ensure that you are involved in all aspects of the technique to be able to claim that the research is your work shared with others.

1. Stream location:

- choose a stream that is not too wide, too deep or shallow, too fast-flowing or tidal
- ensure that you can gain easy access to the stream (you may need to ask permission)
- identify a section of a stream that allows for changes in the measured criteria (e.g. channel size, discharge) and includes features that could influence flow and discharge (e.g. tributaries, changes in slope or land use).

2. Sampling strategy (review the guidance on p. 9):

- Once you have decided the length of the stream section, then you need to decide the number of sample points. You have to consider:
  - how much data needs to be gathered to test any hypothesis (e.g. the Spearman rank correlation coefficient needs at least ten pairs of data)
  - that it may take at least one hour to gather the data at each sample point
  - that working in groups allows more sample points/data to be collected
  - the benefits of repeat visits/sampling to allow for comparison of the gathered data over time, or following an event on the stream, such as after heavy rainfall.

What to measure

1. Channel width – the distance from one bank to the other can be measured just above the water level.
2. Bankfull width – taken at obvious breaks in the slope of both banks. By securing a horizontal line across the stream channel you can identify and measure the maximum volume of water that the channel can hold.
3. Bankfull depth – the vertical distance between the water level and the line representing the bankfull width. This should not vary across the river.

contd

VIDEO LINK 

Check out the videos at www.brightredbooks.net for additional information on river landscapes.

ONLINE 

Check out the web pages at www.brightredbooks.net, which will provide you with ideas and practical advice.

ONLINE 

Follow the link at www.brightredbooks.net for more information on the Bradshaw model.

ONLINE 

Find a great example, Ashes Hollow River, at www.brightredbooks.net

VIDEO LINK 

Watch the video at www.brightredbooks.net on how to measure stream width.

Measuring bankfull width.

VIDEO LINK 

Watch the video at www.brightredbooks.net on how to measure stream depth.

4. Channel depth – measure the depth of the stream by resting a metre stick on the bed of the stream, with the thin side facing upstream, at regular intervals.
5. Wetted perimeter – this is the total distance for which the river water is in contact with the bed and banks at a given cross section.

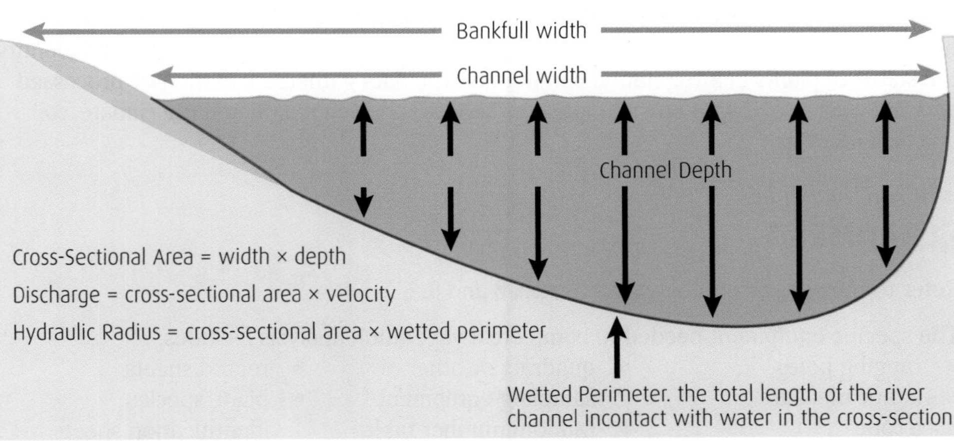

Stream measurements.

6. Flow velocity – ideally use a flow meter (i.e. a hydro-prop with the propeller facing upstream) at the same points as the depth survey. You could also use a float (e.g. an orange) and see how long it takes to go a set distance of 5–10 m.
7. River discharge – the discharge of a river is the volume of water which flows through it in a given time. It is usually measured in cubic metres per second. The volume of the discharge will be determined by factors such as climate, vegetation, soil type, drainage basin relief and human activity.

CONSIDERATIONS AND LIMITATIONS

Refer to the considerations and limitations section for beach-profile analysis, microclimate analysis and slope analysis.

Pay particular attention to your personal safety when working in or near water. Follow the advice in the various video links on these pages.

Check out the methodology on pp. 16 and 17 on how to measure the long profile of a stream.

THINGS TO DO AND THINK ABOUT

Refer to the generic advice on pp. 8 and 9 and the following specific points.

Think about the possible links that stream analysis has with other geographical techniques in this study guide. For example:

- combining stream analysis with pebble analysis and slope analysis to compare two different sections of the same stream or similar sections of two different streams (pp. 10–23)
- combining stream analysis, microclimate analysis and vegetation analysis with perception studies and interviews to investigate the perception that a river can be both an opportunity and a threat to a settlement (pp. 24–37)
- statistical testing, such as the Spearman rank correlation coefficient (pp. 38–53)
- graphical techniques, such as scatter graphs (pp. 54–63)
- mapping techniques, such as annotations, cross-sections, transects and isovels (pp. 64–81).

VIDEO LINK

Watch this video at www.brightredbooks.net on how to measure a wetted perimeter.

VIDEO LINK

Watch the video at www.brightredbooks.net on how to measure velocity.

VIDEO LINK

Check out the clip at www.brightredbooks.net on how to measure a river.

ONLINE

You could use the link at www.brightredbooks.net to calculate discharge.

VIDEO LINK

Check out the videos at www.brightredbooks.net for information on Juggaer Beck and Broxa.

DON'T FORGET

Review your recorded data sheets to ensure they are complete.

DON'T FORGET

Evaluate your research and consider whether the data collected is sufficient to meet the needs of your initial research questions. If not, you may have to carry out further field research.

ONLINE

Check out the links and videos at www.brightredbooks.net to practise your skills.

ONLINE TEST

Test yourself on this topic at www.brightredbooks.net

VEGETATION ANALYSIS

PURPOSE

Geographers are interested in the way plants adapt and respond to different environments. The microclimate, altitude, aspect, soil type, and the interaction of humans and animals all have noticeable and measurable effects on the type and condition of vegetation in an area. It is necessary to gather information during fieldwork activities to characterise and identify the status of plants in a vegetation community. The data gathered can then be processed and analysed to highlight any relationships between the vegetation and the climate, soil and other factors.

ONLINE 

Check out the websites at www.brightredbooks.net for some ideas and suggestions.

VIDEO LINK 

Check out the videos on sampling techniques at www.brightredbooks.net

EQUIPMENT

Refer to the generic equipment list on pp. 8 and 9.

The specific equipment needed to complete a vegetation analysis includes:

- ranging poles
- a tape measure
- a rope
- a compass
- quadrats or other sampling equipment
- random number tables (if needed)
- record sheets
- plant/species identification sheets.

ONLINE 

Check out the websites about how to conduct vegetation analysis using sampling at www.brightredbooks.net

METHODOLOGY

Refer to the generic advice on pp. 8 and 9, especially about sampling methods, and the following specific points.

This technique is, by its nature, a group activity. You must ensure that you are involved in all aspects of the technique to be able to claim that the research is your work shared with others.

Check out similar methodologies used on pp. 10 and 11 (beach-profile analysis), pp. 12 and 13 (microclimate analysis), pp. 16 and 17 (slope analysis) and pp. 18 and 19 (soil analysis).

VIDEO LINK 

Check out the videos on how to use a quadrat at www.brightredbooks.net

Vegetation sampling

The sampling method should be appropriate for the vegetation and the environment.

Where you are investigating:

- a gradient with a steady change in soil, microclimate or altitude, you can use systematic sampling along a transect with samples collected at regular distances of altitudes, such as changes through a wood, across a sand dune/salt marsh or a footpath
- over a short distance, such as 30 m, the sampling may be continuous
- in a landscape with no gradient, random sampling is used to compare two contrasting areas
- in an area that is not uniform, such as a woodland with two distinct ages of trees, it is necessary to stratify the sampling method with a number of samples taken from each area according to the relative size of the areas
- in an area where the vegetation species grow in clumps or clusters, you should use stratified sampling because some species could be missed if you simply use random sampling.

VIDEO LINK 

Watch the videos on how to set up a transect at www.brightredbooks.net

ONLINE 

Check out the websites at www.brightredbooks.net about why and how to use transects.

Sampling using a quadrat.

Quadrat

The term 'quadrat' can refer to:

- a square or rectangular plot of land used to mark a physical area at random to isolate a sample and to determine the percentage of vegetation and animals occurring within the marked area
- a tool used in ecology for sampling purposes – for instance, a quadrat is placed on the ground at random to count the number of vegetation species within the sample.

ONLINE 

Check out the links at www.brightredbooks.net for help on identifying plants and trees.

contd

Transect

A transect is a line across a habitat or part of a habitat. It can be as simple as a string or rope placed in a line on the ground. The number of each plant species can be observed and recorded at regular intervals along the transect.

Check out how to set up a transect on pp. 11 and 12 (beach-profile analysis), pp. 16 and 17 (slope analysis) and pp. 18 and 19 (soil analysis).

Sampling using a line transect.

Plant identification

A key skill within vegetation analysis is to identify the plant and/or tree species present.

PUTTING THE TECHNIQUES INTO PRACTICE

Sand-dune succession

This is the evolution of plant communities at a site over time from pioneer species to climax vegetation.

CONSIDERATIONS AND LIMITATIONS

Refer to the 'considerations and limitations' sections for beach-profile analysis, microclimate analysis and slope analysis as well as the following points.

- carry out a vegetation analysis when the plants are visible and growing
- leaves, as well as flowers, are useful in identifying plants
- if you are not sure about a plant species, take photographs to help identify it later
- putting a white paper collar around the leaf/flower will give a clearer photograph (do not pick wild flowers and leaves)
- vegetation analysis combines a range of techniques, including the use of sampling techniques, quadrats, transects and plant species identification
- the recorded data from a vegetation analysis can be plotted on a graph showing plant type, height change and the change for each section – the graph can then be annotated with any points of interest, such as areas of the sections in which plants would not grow properly, evidence of erosion or different vegetation cover.

THINGS TO DO AND THINK ABOUT

Refer to the generic advice on pp. 8 and 9 and the following specific points.

Think about the possible links that vegetation analysis has with other geographical techniques in this study guide. For example:

- combining vegetation analysis with beach-profile analysis, microclimate analysis, pebble analysis, slope analysis and soil analysis to compare the vegetation along different transects across a sand-dune coastline or between a north-facing and south-facing hill slope (pp. 10–23)
- combining slope analysis and vegetation analysis with interviews, questionnaires and rural land-use mapping to investigate the environmental and ecological impact of modern farming practices (pp. 24–37)
- statistical testing, such as the standard deviation of the number of trees per hectare, or the chi-squared test (pp. 38–53)
- graphical techniques, such as kite graphs and dispersion diagrams (pp. 54–63)
- mapping techniques, such as annotations and transects (pp. 64–81).

VIDEO LINK

Check out the videos at www.brightredbooks.net to acquire knowledge about the formation and characteristics of sand dunes.

ONLINE

Check out the websites at www.brightredbooks.net for detailed information on sand-dune succession.

ONLINE

Check out the link at www.brightredbooks.net for practical help in carrying out sand-dune succession fieldwork and ecological succession.

ONLINE

Check out the websites at www.brightredbooks.net for further considerations and limitations.

DON'T FORGET

Evaluate your research and consider whether the data collected is sufficient to meet the needs of your initial research questions. If not, you may have to carry out further field research.

ONLINE TEST

Test yourself on vegetation analysis on our Digital Zone at www.brightredbooks.net

VIDEO LINK

Check out the video at www.brightredbooks.net to see how to calculate the dispersion of a sample set.

ONLINE

Follow the link at www.brightredbooks.net on how to calculate biodiversity.

ENVIRONMENTAL-QUALITY SURVEYS

ONLINE 

Check out the links at www.brightredbooks.net for some ideas and suggestions.

PURPOSE

Environmental-quality surveys are used to measure the 'look and feel' of a location. It is a subjective technique in which one person may think a location is very noisy, but another person may think that the same location is OK in terms of noise levels.

Environmental-quality surveys are based on using a set of broad criteria on which to make a judgement about a location, such as

- the quality of buildings
- the amount of traffic
- local shops
- the services available
- the general quality of the area.

GENERAL QUALITY						
Negative	1 (or −2)	2 (or −1)	3 (or 0)	4 (or +1)	5 (or +2)	Positive
Much litter						No litter
Paths poorly maintained/broken paving						Paths well maintained
Area is undesirable						Area is desirable
Unwelcoming feel						Welcoming feeling
Total score – general quality =						

Extract example of a bipolar survey.

As can be seen from the table, the criterion – in this instance general quality – is further subdivided into a range of matching pairs, one negative and the other positive. Each pair is assessed on a scale from 1 to 5, with 1 being the most negative and 5 the most positive. Alternatively, the scale may be from −2 to +2.

EQUIPMENT

Refer to the generic equipment list on pp. 8 and 9.

The specific equipment needed to complete an environmental-quality survey includes:

- prepared survey sheets, such as bipolar surveys
- base maps of the area
- a digital camera
- sketching materials.

METHODOLOGY

Refer to the generic advice on pp. 8 and 9, especially about sampling methods, and the following specific points.

This technique may be completed as a group activity. You must ensure that you are involved in all aspects of the technique to be able to claim that the research is your work shared with others.

Check out the methodologies used on pp. 26 and 27 (interview design and implementation), pp. 30 and 31 (perception studies), pp. 32 and 33 (questionnaire design and implementation) and p. 56 (bipolar analysis).

DON'T FORGET 

Build up a good personal knowledge of the area prior to your fieldwork to develop relevant and detailed criteria for the survey.

ONLINE 

Check out the website about sampling techniques at www.brightredbooks.net

Using a bipolar survey

1. Decide the context of the survey.

Environmental-quality surveys can be used in a number of contexts, such as carrying out a survey on:

- a number of separate locations within one area (e.g. a central business district or residential area)

contd

- two or more areas (e.g. inner-city housing versus suburbs)
- locations along a transect/transects (pp. 80 and 81) (e.g. from the central business district to the urban fringe)
- two shopping areas (e.g. two city-centre shopping streets or two shopping malls)
- a tourist area/resort (e.g. a seaside resort or between two country parks).

2. Decide your sampling method (e.g. random or regular).
3. Decide the criteria you are going to use (your choice), such as the quality of buildings, the amount of traffic, local shops, available services and the general quality of the area. For each criterion, choose pairs of opposite characteristics, such as much litter and no litter, and associate these with a scale score from 1 to 5 or −2 to +2 (1/−2 very negative, 5/+2 very positive). The number of pairs you select is your choice. Put them in a table with the list of negative environmental qualities on the left and the positive environmental qualities on the right. Between the two, have five columns headed 1, 2, 3, 4, 5 or −2, −1, 0, +1, +2.

If you intend to use a pre-printed example, check carefully that the criteria and the pairs are suitable for the locations you intend to survey.

Prepare a copy of the survey table for each site to be visited.

4. Trial run. Having decided on your bipolar pairs for all the criteria, print off two examples and select two locations: one that you think is really nice and the other not so nice. Trial the survey to see if the nice area comes out with a high score and the other area with a low score. You might decide at this point that some of the criteria, or pairs, do not really help to differentiate between the locations, and your survey sheet needs to be amended.
5. Decide whether you are going to complete the survey yourself, or whether you are going to ask someone else, or a random selection of people, to complete it. The choice will have an effect on the ratings. If you repeat the survey yourself, then you are more likely to rate each area using the same judgement. Other people may be more subjective.

CONSIDERATIONS AND LIMITATIONS

This survey technique is based on making judgements. The judgement may well be based on wide-ranging, impartial and detailed information supported by experience, understanding and evidence, but more often than not judgements are based on stereotypes or misconceptions – for example, rural areas are safer than urban areas.

It is worth comparing the results from such surveys with published data (e.g. census data or house prices).

THINGS TO DO AND THINK ABOUT

Refer to the generic advice on pp. 8 and 9 and the following specific points.

Think about the possible links that an environmental-quality survey has with other geographical techniques in this study guide. For example:

- combining an environmental-quality survey with perception studies, interviews, questionnaires and traffic counts to gather data on noise pollution using a decibel meter or night-time light pollution (pp. 24–37)
- combining beach-profile analysis, pebble analysis and vegetation analysis with an environmental-quality survey or perception studies to carry out a beach-quality survey (pp. 10–23)
- statistical testing – for example, you could use the Spearman rank correlation coefficient or the Pearson product moment correlation coefficient to enhance the results of the bipolar analysis (pp. 38–53)
- graphical techniques, such as bipolar analysis (pp. 54–63)
- mapping techniques, such as the annotation of maps, photographs and transects (pp. 64–81).

ONLINE

Check out the links at www.brightredbooks.net for further examples of survey sheets.

ONLINE

Find a printable example of an environmental-quality survey sheet www.brightredbooks.net

ONLINE

Check out the links at www.brightredbooks.net for further considerations and limitations.

DON'T FORGET

Evaluate your research and consider whether the data collected is sufficient to meet the needs of your initial research questions. If not, you may have to carry out further field research.

ONLINE TEST

Test yourself on environmental-quality surveys on our Digital Zone at www.brightredbooks.net

INTERVIEW DESIGN AND IMPLEMENTATION

DON'T FORGET

You may have to tailor the questions to suit who is being interviewed.

ONLINE

Check out the websites at www.brightredbooks.net for some ideas and suggestions about interview design and implementation.

VIDEO LINK

Check out the videos on how to carry out interviews at www.brightredbooks.net

PURPOSE

Conducting face-to-face interviews is a good way of collecting data that may not be available from other sources. Interviews can be used to:

- find out people's values and opinions on local issues by carrying out street interviews
- ask questions of a representative of an organisation who can give some insight into a decision-making process and provide specific details.

If you are researching a planning issue, such as the siting of a new shopping centre or supermarket extension, you might interview several people, including:

- the manager of the shopping centre/supermarket to provide a commercial viewpoint
- the local planning officer to provide information relating to the local plan
- a local councillor to provide a political view/opinion on the likely impacts
- local residents to gauge their opinions on the proposal.

EQUIPMENT

Refer to the generic equipment list on pp. 8 and 9.

The specific equipment needed to design and carry out an interview includes:

- prepared interview questions
- recording sheets
- an audio recorder
- an identity badge or brief letter.

METHODOLOGY

Refer to the generic advice on pp. 8 and 9, especially about sampling methods, and the following specific points.

This technique may, in part, be completed as a group activity. You must ensure that you are involved in all aspects of the technique to be able to claim that the research is your work shared with others.

Check out the methodologies used on pp. 24 and 25 (environmental-quality surveys), pp. 30 and 31 (perception studies) and pp. 32–33 (questionnaire design and implementation).

Interview design

As with all research, good planning is important. In the case of interviews, you need to carry out the following steps.

1. Do some background research on the topic.
2. Develop a set of questions that will allow you to gather information to answer your research question(s). The questions should be unambiguous and open-ended, structured not to produce a simple yes or no, and sequenced in such a way as to build up information and lead on to the next question. You should trial the questions with friends and family to ensure they have the right tone – the interviewee is doing you a favour, so you don't want the question to sound rude or to give a poor impression.
3. Be prepared to ask supplementary questions if appropriate.
4. If working with someone else, make sure you have agreed and use the same questions.
5. Have a short and simple statement to present to the interviewee about what you are doing and why.

Interview implementation

Planning interviews: identify people to interview.

If you are conducting a street interview, select a suitable location to politely stop people and ask your questions. Show them your badge or letter and explain simply what you want. You will only have a limited time to ask questions, so focus on the main issues and the most appropriate/pertinent questions.

You cannot interview everyone, so decide on a suitable sampling technique, such as:

- systematic sampling – every tenth person
- random sampling – choose people using random number tables
- stratified sampling – depending on the context of the research, you could target a particular age group or ensure equal numbers of respondents from each age group.

Interviewing a named person in an organisation (e.g. a park warden or the manager of a visitor centre) provides an opportunity to ask more searching and detailed questions of people who may have influenced or have been part of a decision-making process.

contd

Write a formal letter to the person(s) you wish to interview, including the following details:

- an explanation of who you are and the purpose of the interview(s)
- a selection of flexible dates and times for the interview – the people you want to interview will have tight schedules and will need to plan well in advance
- indicate how long the interview might take
- make clear what use will be made of the information
- provide contact details (e.g. address, mobile number and e-mail address).

You need to wait for a reply to your letter. If the person agrees, you need to formalise a place time and date. If you receive no response, you might consider a follow-up call and, if that also fails, then choose another person to interview and start again. Once the interview date/time has been set, you might consider sending the interviewee the questions in advance.

Conducting the interview

Remember the following when conducting the interview:

- make sure you have all the equipment you need, including spare batteries for any recording equipment, and writing materials
- dress appropriately, act politely and don't overstay your welcome – 30 minutes should be enough time to obtain the information
- some people may dislike being recorded, so be prepared to write their responses down
- listen carefully to the answers given and be prepared to politely ask further probing questions
- at the end of the interview, thank the person for their time and cooperation and, in addition, write to thank them for participating.

CONSIDERATIONS AND LIMITATIONS

Refer to the 'considerations and limitations' section for questionnaire design and implementation as well as the following points.

It is difficult to carry out a statistical analysis of the results from an interview. Interviews are a more flexible way of gathering information than questionnaires by allowing:

- you to ask longer, less structured, more detailed and open-ended questions
- the interviewee to express their feelings and opinions beyond the structure of set questions
- you to ask supplementary questions based on their responses.

THINGS TO DO AND THINK ABOUT

Refer to the generic advice on pp. 8 and 9 and the following specific points. Think about the possible links that interview design and implementation have with other geographical techniques in this study guide. For example:

- combining interviews with questionnaires, pedestrian surveys and traffic surveys to gather data on the effectiveness of park-and-ride schemes (pp. 24–37)
- combining microclimate analysis with environmental-quality surveys, interviews and perception studies to analysis differences in people's use of a landscape (pp. 10–23)
- statistical testing (pp. 38–53)
- graphical techniques, such as 'talking heads' to represent the range of values and attitudes (pp. 54–63)
- mapping techniques, such as annotations of photographs to set the scene (pp. 64–81).

ONLINE

Check out the website on how to write a formal letter at www.brightredbooks.net

ONLINE

Check out the websites at www.brightredbooks.net for further considerations and limitations.

DON'T FORGET

Be prepared for people to refuse to be interviewed or to refuse to answer challenging questions.

DON'T FORGET

Evaluate your research and consider whether the data collected is sufficient to meet the needs of your initial research questions. If not, you may have to carry out further field research.

ONLINE TEST

Test yourself on our Digital Zone at www.brightredbooks.net

VIDEO LINK

Check out the video at www.brightredbooks.net on how to complete qualitative analysis of interview data.

DATA-GATHERING TECHNIQUES

PEDESTRIAN SURVEYS AND TRAFFIC SURVEYS

PURPOSE

These are separate techniques with a common purpose and methodology.

Pedestrian and traffic surveys, or counts, are techniques used to find out how and why the density and movement of pedestrians or traffic varies in different parts of an urban environment. You would expect an increase in the number of pedestrians and traffic the nearer you are to the central business district.

ONLINE 

Check out the websites at www.brightredbooks.net for some ideas and suggestions about pedestrian and traffic surveys.

VIDEO LINK 

Check out the videos at www.brightredbooks.net from further information and advice.

EQUIPMENT

Refer to the generic equipment list on pp. 8 and 9.

The specific equipment needed to complete a pedestrian/traffic survey includes:

- a click counter(s), or use tally marks
- a town-centre map
- recording sheets.

Click counter

METHODOLOGY

Refer to the generic advice on pp. 8 and 9, especially about sampling methods, and the following specific points – for example, sampling points and timings need to be decided along the transects (pp. 80 and 81) or sites across an urban area.

These techniques are, by their nature, a group activity. You must ensure that you are involved in all aspects of the techniques to be able to claim that the research is your work shared with others. Conducting fieldwork in a large group means that a time could be set whereby each group counts the number of pedestrians/vehicles that pass a certain point at a pre-determined time.

Check out similar methodologies used on pp. 24 and 25 (environmental-quality surveys), pp. 30 and 31 (perception studies), pp. 26 and 27 (interview design and implementation), pp. 32 and 33 (questionnaire design and implementation), pp. 34 and 35 (rural land-use mapping) and pp. 36 and 37 (urban land-use mapping).

Main shopping street

Pedestrian/traffic survey/count

- location: a range of sites within the city/town centre, including: along main roads with major junctions/crossroads – roundabouts are good locations for recording the relative distribution of vehicles coming off a main road; minor roads to highlight the fall-off in numbers close to busy areas; and passages and paths
- time: both peak and off-peak times
- frequency: over a number of different days/weeks/months for comparative purposes – one-off sampling is suspect and may lead to unreliable results
- under different weather conditions.

ONLINE 

An alternative option for conducting a pedestrian survey/count can be found at www.brightredbooks.net

Pedestrian survey/count

Count the number of people (footfall count) who pass by a fixed point of your choice at each site during a 15–20-minute period. The count must be taken at the same time and duration at all sites. Work in pairs, covering both sides of a route, and count people moving in both directions.

contd

Pedestrianised areas are challenging to count because the number of people will be large and people may be hanging about rather than moving in a particular direction. You may decide to avoid pedestrianised sites because they may show biased results. You will need to devise a strategy for this before you start – for example, select a line of sight and only count those people who cross this line.

Traffic survey/count

Choose a position to do the count that gives you a clear viewpoint without obstructing/distracting road users.

Count the number of vehicles that pass by a fixed point of your choice at each site during a 15–20-minute period. The count must be taken at the same time and duration at all sites.

Work in pairs, covering both sides of a route, and count the vehicles moving in both directions. Be clear about the direction of movement – one-way streets are easy.

Record the data on a tally sheet. An example can be found on the Digital Zone.

CONSIDERATIONS AND LIMITATIONS

Even using multiple sample points and timings of pedestrian and traffic surveys/counts, it may well be impossible to fully explain the complex dynamic nature of the movements of people and traffic within a built-up area.

In the interests of personal safety and to cover the volumes of traffic that may pass a site, work in pairs.

You could combine a traffic count with:

- an estimation of car and bus occupancy rates
- the home base of commercial vehicles – these are often printed on the side or back of lorries/vans
- work out the approximate traffic speed using two fixed points – do a time/distance calculation, such as:

$$\text{Average speed } (S) = \frac{\text{total distance travelled } (D)}{\text{time to travel this distance } (T)}$$

THINGS TO DO AND THINK ABOUT

Refer to the generic advice on pp. 8 and 9 and the following specific points.

Think about the possible links that pedestrian and traffic surveys/counts have with other geographical techniques in this study guide. For example:

- combining pedestrian and/or traffic counts with interviews, questionnaires and perception studies to gather data on traffic trouble spots, public-transport issues and route-quality surveys (pp. 24–37)
- combining slope analysis and vegetation analysis with pedestrian survey, interviews and questionnaires to gather data on footpath maintenance, usage and connectivity within a recreational area (pp. 10–23)
- statistical testing, such as measures of central tendency and measures of dispersion, the chi-squared test and the Spearman rank correlation coefficient (pp. 38–53)
- graphical techniques – such as divided bar graphs and dispersion diagrams (pp. 54–63)
- mapping techniques, such as annotations, flow maps and transects (pp. 64–81).

DON'T FORGET

In the interests of personal safety and to cover the volumes of traffic that may pass a site, work in pairs.

DON'T FORGET

Evaluate your research and consider whether the data collected is sufficient to meet the needs of your initial research questions. If not, you may have to carry out further field research.

ONLINE TEST

Test yourself on pedestrian and traffic surveys/counts on our Digital Zone at www.brightredbooks.net

VIDEO LINK

Check out the video on how to use pictograms at www.brightredbooks.net

ONLINE

Check out the websites at www.brightredbooks.net for further considerations and limitations.

PERCEPTION STUDIES

DON'T FORGET 

Perception studies involve assessing the quality of an area or facility using a mix of criteria.

ONLINE 

Check out the websites at www.brightredbooks.net for some ideas and suggestions about perception studies.

PURPOSE

Perception is defined as a belief or opinion, often held by many people and based on how things seem – for example, 'there is a general perception that exams are becoming easier to pass'. However, perceptions are subjective and variable. Two people who see the same event may well have a different perception of that event.

The way we perceive things is influenced by a number of factors, including:

- age
- gender
- cultural background
- past experiences
- family upbringing
- personality
- education
- peer-group pressures
- our mood – how you feel at the time.

EQUIPMENT

Refer to the generic equipment list on pp. 8 and 9.

The specific equipment needed to complete a perception study includes:

- base maps of the area
- a digital camera
- sketching materials
- prepared survey sheets (e.g. mental maps)
- resources to draw mental maps.

METHODOLOGY

Refer to the generic advice on pp. 8 and 9, especially about sampling methods, and the following specific points.

This technique is, by its nature, a group activity. You must ensure that you are involved in all aspects of the technique to be able to claim that the research is your work shared with others.

Check out similar methodologies used on pp. 24 and 25 (environmental-quality survey), pp. 26 and 27 (interview design and implementation), pp. 32 and 33 (questionnaire design and implementation), pp. 34 and 35 (rural land-use mapping) and pp. 36 and 37 (urban land-use mapping).

Perception studies fall into the following three categories.

1. How people perceive space.

- Mental maps – this is a valuable method to show how people structure space in their minds and know about their surroundings. The map in our mind is not the same as an OS map. A mental map is made up of five elements:
  - paths – the routes along which we move
  - edges – barriers around areas (e.g. woods and railways)
  - nodes – places where people cluster
  - landmarks – distinctive features
  - districts – identifiable residential areas.

  Areas with these five elements are easier for people to map.
- Subjective distance – people often perceive unfamiliar locations to be further away than familiar locations. The distance to unfamiliar locations is further exaggerated if people have a pre-conceived negative perception of the location.

contd

2. How people evaluate their environment.
   - Hazard perception – many people live in areas prone to flooding, and their perception of the threat is influenced by their past experience. Research has found that people who have experienced floods are more likely to underestimate potential risk or damage.
   - Levels of crime – you can produce a 'map of fear' by asking people to perceive how safe they feel in an area. The results can be compared with actual crime data.
   - Residential preference – why do people prefer one area? Certain attributes, such as climate and employment prospects, produce positive perceptions of an area.
   - Knowledge of an area – you can compare the level of knowledge with the length of time people have stayed in an area, their age, income, education and mobility – this could be part of a study on the use of recreational resources.
   - Landscape evaluation – aim to give landscapes an objective score. This score is then used to assess the impact of an environmental change, such as building a new road.
3. How people make decisions.

   Perception studies are useful in determining the reason why people make decisions, such as the building of a new road or the siting of a fast-food outlet.

ONLINE

Check out the Digital Zone to find further advice and guidance on perception studies.

CONSIDERATIONS AND LIMITATIONS

Perception studies can be undertaken on their own but are more likely to be used in conjunction with other techniques, such as an environmental-quality survey, a pedestrian survey, a traffic survey, and interviews or questionnaires. Refer to the considerations and limitations of these techniques.

Perception studies can produce simplistic and unconvincing conclusions unless you take care to follow some basic guidelines:

- use criteria that will allow you to research the topic – for example, research into deprivation will use a range of socio-economic criteria, such as employment, family structure, mobility and health
- weight the more important criteria more heavily – for example, unemployment has a direct effect on deprivation, so it might be given a weighting of 2 or 3
- you need to be objective and non-biased and to produce a scoring system not influenced by gender or culture
- provide written descriptors when using a bipolar analysis.

ONLINE

Check out the links at www.brightredbooks.net for further considerations and limitations.

DON'T FORGET

Mental maps are impossible to analyse statistically to confirm the value of the data.

DON'T FORGET

Evaluate your research and consider whether the data collected is sufficient to meet the needs of your initial research questions. If not, you may have to carry out further field research.

THINGS TO DO AND THINK ABOUT

Refer to the generic advice on pp. 8 and 9 and the following specific points.

Think about the possible links that perception studies have with other geographical techniques in this study guide:

- combining perception studies with interviews and questionnaires to compare two adjacent, but contrasting, residential areas, or one area within a National Park with another outside (pp. 24–37)
- combining vegetation analysis with perception studies, interviews and questionnaires to gather data on the effectiveness of management strategies at a conservation site (pp. 10–23)
- statistical testing, such as measures of central tendency and measures of dispersion and the chi-squared test (pp. 38–53)
- graphical techniques, such as divided bar graphs and bipolar analysis (pp. 54–63)
- mapping techniques, such as annotations, choropleth maps, isoline maps and flow maps (pp. 64–81).

ONLINE TEST

Test yourself on perception studies on our Digital Zone at www.brightredbooks.net

QUESTIONNAIRE DESIGN AND IMPLEMENTATION

PURPOSE

Questionnaires allow you to gather primary data, which may not be available from other sources, on your choice of topic using pre-determined questions. Questionnaires can be used to collect the following types of data:

- population characteristics, such as age, gender and occupation
- spatial patterns, such as origins of visitors and travel patterns
- patterns of behaviour, such as shopping habits, travel preferences and recreational activities
- views and opinions on local issues, such as a proposed traffic bypass system.

There are two types of questionnaire:

- face-to-face surveys carried out in the street using closed questions requiring short responses
- drop-and-collect surveys, with questionnaires delivered with a covering letter and collected some time later – this allows more open-ended questions, but the return rate may be as low as 10%.

If you were researching a planning issue, such as the siting of a new hospital or the need to extend an existing recreational facility, you might ask for questionnaires to be completed by several groups of people:

- face-to-face questionnaires
  - local residents to gauge their opinions on the proposal
  - users of existing facilities.
- drop-and-collect questionnaires
  - a manager/operator of the proposed development
  - the local planning officer to provide information relating to the local plan
  - a local councillor to provide a political view/opinion on the likely effects.

DON'T FORGET

Research suggests that people often respond with the answers they think you want to hear.

ONLINE

Check out the links at www.brightredbooks.net for some ideas and suggestions about questionnaire design and implementation.

EQUIPMENT

Refer to the generic equipment list on pp. 8 and 9.

The specific equipment needed to design and implement a questionnaire includes:

- prepared questionnaires
- an identity badge or letter.

METHODOLOGY

Refer to the generic advice on pp. 8 and 9, especially about sampling methods, and the following specific points.

This technique may be, in part, completed as a group activity. You must ensure that you are involved in all aspects of the technique to be able to claim that the research is your work shared with others.

Check out the methodologies used on pp. 24 and 25 (environmental-quality survey), pp. 26 and 27 (interview design and implementation) and pp. 30 and 31 (perception studies).

Questionnaire design

A well-designed questionnaire requires thought and effort. It needs to be planned and developed in a number of stages. Trial your questionnaire with 10–20 people to identify any issues and then amend or adapt the questions as necessary.

contd

ONLINE

Check out the websites at www.brightredbooks.net for advice and guidance on how to design a questionnaire.

ONLINE

Check out the videos at www.brightredbooks.net for some ideas and suggestions about questionnaire design and implementation.

Questionnaire implementation

You first need to decide:

- when and where you are going to conduct the questionnaire
- a suitable sampling strategy, such as systematic sampling (e.g. every tenth person), random sampling (choose people using random number tables) or stratified sampling, which is necessary to sample all parts of a population
- the sample size (e.g. at least 50, possibly up to 100 people).

Conducting the questionnaire

Make sure you have all the equipment you need.

- Face-to-face questionnaire – select a suitable location to politely stop and ask your questions. Not everyone you select will accept your invitation. You will only have a limited time to ask questions, so focus on the most appropriate/pertinent issues.
- Drop-and-collect questionnaire – drop and collect the questionnaire at pre-arranged times. You should include a letter explaining the purpose of the questionnaire and how it should be completed. Give the person time to complete the questionnaire. You might follow up the questionnaire delivery with a reminder call/e-mail.

Thank people for their time and cooperation. For drop-and-collect questionnaires, you might produce a thank-you letter to deliver at the time of collection.

Follow-up activities

Go through each respondent's questionnaire in turn, adding in the codes. Enter this data into a spreadsheet. See the Digital Zone for an example of what this might look like.

CONSIDERATIONS AND LIMITATIONS

Refer to the 'considerations and limitations' section for interview design and implementation as well as the following points.

Questionnaire design and implementation can be undertaken on its own, but questionnaires are more likely to be used in conjunction with other techniques, such as an environmental-quality survey, perception studies, a pedestrian survey, a traffic survey, interviews, rural land-use mapping and urban land-use mapping.

THINGS TO DO AND THINK ABOUT

Refer to the generic advice on pp. 8 and 9 and the following specific points.

Think about the possible links that questionnaire design and implementation surveys have with other geographical techniques in this study guide, such as:

- combining questionnaires with interviews, perception studies and urban land-use mapping to gather data to determine if and why certain shops avoid city centres (pp. 24–37)
- combining beach-profile analysis, slope analysis and vegetation analysis with perception studies, interviews and questionnaires to gather data on the impact of coastal protection schemes (pp. 10–23)
- statistical testing is possible depending on the nature of the data – for example, cross-tabulating the results, measurements of central tendency and measures of dispersion, and the chi-squared test (pp. 38–53)
- graphical techniques, such as pie charts and bar graphs (pp. 54–63)
- mapping techniques – it is possible to map some data (e.g. annotations, choropleth maps, isoline maps and flow maps) (pp. 64–81).

ONLINE

Follow the link at www.brightredbooks.net to read how to write a formal letter.

VIDEO LINK

Check out the videos at www.brightredbooks.net to see how the gathered data may be analysed.

ONLINE

Head to www.brightredbooks.net to find further advice on how to design and carry out a questionnaire.

ONLINE

Check out the websites at www.brightredbooks.net for further considerations and limitations.

DON'T FORGET

Be prepared for people to refuse to be interviewed or to refuse to answer challenging questions.

DON'T FORGET

Evaluate your research and consider whether the data collected is sufficient to meet the needs of your initial research questions. If not, you may have to carry out further field research.

ONLINE TEST

Test yourself on our Digital Zone at www.brightredbooks.net

RURAL LAND-USE MAPPING

PURPOSE

This technique is about mapping land-use types within a rural environment. The completed map will show the types and intensities of land use in an area.

In carrying out this technique, you need to:

- identify a list of the likely land-use categories to be found in a rural environment, such as forestry, agriculture, settlement and transport (see table)
- configure a classification (key symbol and colour coding) system to map these rural land-use categories (see table below).

DON'T FORGET 

You can adapt the land-use classification key to suit the needs of the research.

CATEGORY	SUB-CATEGORIES AND KEY	COLOUR CODE
Forestry	c = coniferous, d = deciduous, m = mixed, co = commercial, nc = non-commercial	Green
Agriculture	ca = cropped arable (you could include sub-categories for each crop), uc = uncropped arable (set-aside land), g = grassland, of = other farmland (e.g. buildings), mg = market garden, o = orchards	Brown
Open space	h = heath, m = moorland, rg = rough grazing	Purple
Residential	h = hamlet, v = village; see also urban land-use classification key	Grey
Industrial/commercial	q = quarry, m = mine, fp = food-processing	Blue
Recreational	gc = golf course, ec = equestrian centre	Red
Transport	roads, railways, rights of way	Yellow
Water features	rivers, lakes, canals	Orange

Example rural land-use classification table.

The first step is to source/produce a base map on which to record the gathered data/information – for example:

- detailed street maps from local councils
- OS maps
- Goad plans.

Rural land-use mapping is a useful technique and is often used in conjunction with other geographical techniques (e.g. annotations, environmental-quality surveys, interviews, questionnaires) to research a variety of rural land-use issues, including:

- conflicting rural land uses, such as between farming practices and land conservation
- changes in rural land use over time, such as comparing current data with historical data to evaluate the urbanisation of rural settlements
- the influence of physical and human factors, such as the location and spacing of settlements and services in a rural area.

ONLINE 

Check out the websites at www.brightredbooks.net for some ideas and suggestions about rural land-use mapping.

ONLINE 

Check out the videos about land-use mapping at www.brightredbooks.net

EQUIPMENT

Refer to the generic equipment list on pp. 8 and 9.

The following specific equipment is needed to complete rural land-use mapping:

- base map of the area (e.g. OS 1:25,000 or Goad plan)
- land-use classification key/code sheet
- digital/mobile phone camera
- coloured pencils.

METHODOLOGY

Refer to the generic advice on pp. 8 and 9, especially about sampling methods, and the following specific points.

This technique may, in part, be completed as a group activity. You must ensure that you are involved in all aspects of the technique to be able to claim that the research is your work shared with others.

contd

Check out the methodologies used on pp. 36–37 for urban land-use mapping.

Step 1: preparation

You need to:

- Decide on the area of study and access an appropriate map to record the gathered data.
- Decide the sampling strategy. If the area being mapped is small, you might be able to map the whole area. However, for a large rural area, you should consider using a transect (pp. 80 and 81). Even this will be a considerable task, so you may also consider sampling land use along the transect line (e.g. every 50 m).

Step 2: gathering data

You may find it useful to use one or more of the following options:

- walk the area/transect and record the gathered data on your base map using the land-use classification sheet
- take digital images of the recorded land use for future reference and use this in support of the completed rural land-use map
- use Google maps (e.g. Street View or satellite images) to check rural land use, including the size of each land-use type, although this method does have its limitations – for example, the view may be out of date.

Step 3: following up

Use all the gathered data to draw a land-use map, colour-coding and annotating as appropriate. You can compare your mapped data with that from other sources.

CONSIDERATIONS AND LIMITATIONS

Obtaining appropriate land-use maps can be expensive. Try a local library, where you might be able to obtain photocopies.

Land-use mapping is a long and laborious task. Take great care to sample appropriately to gather sufficient valid and reliable data.

Although you have a right to access most land and inland waters in Scotland, you have a responsibility to act in the way set out in the Scottish Outdoor Access Code. It might be appropriate to ask permission before accessing farmland.

THINGS TO DO AND THINK ABOUT

Refer to the generic advice on pp. 8 and 9 and the following specific points.

Think about the possible links that rural land-use mapping has with other geographical techniques in this study guide, such as:

- combining rural land-use mapping with interviews, questionnaires and perception studies to determine the perceived, actual and potential conflicts at the urban/rural fringe (pp. 24–37)
- combining slope analysis, soil analysis and vegetation analysis with perception studies, interviews, questionnaires and rural land-use mapping to gather data on the effect of changing farming practices on the environment (pp. 10–23)
- statistical testing is possible depending on the nature of the data, such as cross-tabulating the results for different transects and nearest-neighbour analysis (pp. 38–53)
- graphical techniques, such as pie charts, bar graphs and proportional circles (pp. 54–63)
- mapping techniques, such as annotations, overlays, photographs, sphere-of-influence maps and transect(s) (pp. 64–81).

ONLINE

Follow the links at www.brightredbooks.net for further considerations and limitations.

You can use a smartphone app to record the locations of your sampling points, for example 'Where I am'.

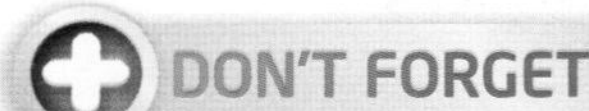

Evaluate your research and consider whether the data collected is sufficient to meet the needs of your initial research questions. If not, you may have to carry out further field research.

ONLINE TEST

Test yourself on, and see examples of, rural land-use mapping on our Digital Zone at www.brightredbooks.net

URBAN LAND-USE MAPPING

PURPOSE

This technique is about mapping land-use types within an urban environment. The completed map will show the types and intensities of land use in an area.

In carrying out this technique, you need to:

- identify a list of the likely land-use categories to be found in an urban environment, such as **R**esidential, **I**ndustrial, **C**ommercial, **E**ntertainment, **P**ublic buildings, **O**pen space, **T**ransport, **S**ervices (**RICEPOTS**) (see table below)
- configure a classification (key symbol and colour coding) system to map the urban land-use categories (see table).

DON'T FORGET

You can also record building height and construction material.

CATEGORY	SUB-CATEGORIES AND KEY	COLOUR CODE
Residential (**R**)	f = flat, t = terraced house, s = semi-detached house, b = bungalow, d = detached house Age: g = Georgian, v = Victorian, iw = interwar, pw = post-war, m = modern	Brown
Industrial (**I**)	l = light manufacturing, h = heavy industry, c = chemical, e = extraction/mining	Grey
Commercial (**C**)	f = food, t = takeaway, p = personal services, d = department store, h = homeware and furniture, g = garage, m = market, s = specialist shop, o = office, v = vacant	Blue
Entertainment(**E**)	h = hotel, s = sports centre, g = gym, t = theatre or cinema, b = bar, r = restaurant or café	Red
Public buildings (**P**)	e = education, l = library, h = hospital, c = place of worship, p = police station, a = ambulance station, f = fire station, w = welfare	Yellow
Open space (**O**)	f = farmland, p = park, c = cemetery, u = unused land, d = derelict building, s = sports field	Green
Transport (**T**)	b = bus station, t = taxi rank, c = car park, r = railway station	Black
Services (**S**)	f = financial, b = business, m = medical, e = estate agent, d = dental	Orange

Example urban land-use classification table.

The first step is to source/produce a base map on which to record the gathered data/information – for example:

- detailed street maps from local councils
- OS maps
- Goad plans.

Urban land-use mapping is a useful technique and is often used in conjunction with other geographical techniques (e.g. annotations, environmental-quality surveys, interviews, questionnaires) to research a variety of urban land-use issues, including:

- conflicting urban land uses, such as the segregation of residential and industrial areas
- changes in urban land use over time, such as comparing your present-day data with historical map data
- changes in urban land use with distance from the central business district, such as identifying changes along a transect (pp. 80 and81) or route from the city centre to the urban fringe.

ONLINE

Head to www.brightredbooks.net for some ideas and suggestions about urban land-use mapping.

VIDEO LINK

Check out the videos about land-use mapping at www.brightredbooks.net

EQUIPMENT

Refer to the generic equipment list on pp. 8 and 9.

The following specific equipment is needed to complete urban land-use mapping:

- base map of the area (e.g. OS 1:25,000 map or Goad plan)
- land-use classification key/code sheet
- a digital/mobile phone camera
- coloured pencils.

METHODOLOGY

Refer to the generic advice on pp. 8 and 9, especially about sampling methods, and the following specific points.

contd

This technique may be, in part, completed as a group activity. You must ensure that you are involved in all aspects of the technique to be able to claim that the research is your work shared with others.

Check out the methodologies used on pp. 34 and 35 for rural land-use mapping.

Step 1: preparation

You need to:

- Decide on the area for the study/transect line/route and access an appropriate map to record your gathered data.
- Decide on the sampling strategy. If the area being mapped is small, you might be able to map the whole area. However, for a large urban area, you should consider using a transect. Even this will be a considerable task, so you may also consider sampling land use along the transect (pp. 80 and 81) (e.g. every 50 m).
- Decide whether you are going to survey both sides of the transect route – that is, both sides of the road.
- Decide whether the recorded land use is at ground level only or also includes the upper floors of buildings.

Step 2: gathering data

You may find it useful to use one or more of the options below:

- walk the area/transect and record the gathered data on your base map using the **RICEPOTS** classification sheet
- take digital images of the recorded land use for future reference and use these in support of the completed urban land-use map
- use Google maps (e.g. Street View and satellite images) to check the urban land use, including the area of each land use in square metres, although this method does have its limitations – for example, the view may be out of date and the building materials may be difficult to determine.

Step 3: following up

Use all the gathered data to draw a land-use map, colour-coding and annotating as appropriate. You can compare your mapped data with that from other sources.

CONSIDERATIONS AND LIMITATIONS

Obtaining appropriate land-use maps can be expensive. Try a local library, where you might be able to obtain photocopies.

Land-use mapping is a long and laborious task. Take great care to sample appropriately to gather sufficient valid and reliable data.

THINGS TO DO AND THINK ABOUT

Refer to the generic advice on pp. 8 and 9 and the following specific points.

Think about the possible links that urban land-use mapping has with other geographical techniques in this study guide, including:

- combining urban land-use mapping with interviews, questionnaires, perception studies, pedestrian surveys and traffic surveys to gather data to determine the impact of an urban fringe retail development on a traditional town centre (pp. 24–37)
- combining beach-profile analysis, slope analysis and vegetation analysis with perception studies, interviews, questionnaires and urban land-use mapping to gather data into the effect of tourism and recreation on a coastal resort (pp. 10–23)
- statistical testing is possible depending on the nature of the data, such as cross-tabulating the results for different transects, mean building heights and the chi-squared test (pp. 38–53)
- graphical techniques, such as pie charts and bar graphs (pp. 54–63)
- mapping techniques, such as annotations, overlays, photographs and transect(s) (pp. 64–81).

ONLINE

Check out the websites at www.brightredbooks.net for further considerations and limitations.

You can use a smartphone app to record the locations of your sampling points, for example 'Where I am'.

Evaluate your research and consider whether the data collected is sufficient to meet the needs of your initial research questions. If not, you may have to carry out further field research.

ONLINE TEST

Test yourself on, and see examples of, urban land-use mapping on our Digital Zone at www.brightredbooks.net

STATISTICS

GENERAL ADVICE ON THE USE OF STATISTICS

PURPOSE

Statistics is the study of the collection, analysis, interpretation, presentation and organisation of data. Different statistical techniques are appropriate in different circumstances and may only be applied to data collected in a particular way. Consequently, when planning to gather data, you have to consider how it should be collected so that it can be processed later by an appropriate statistical method.

The statistical techniques explained on pp. 38–53 are the statistical methodology you are expected to know and understand for the examination. Within the context of the unit on geographical skills and the coursework (the geographical study and geographical issue), you are free to use any appropriate and relevant statistical technique. The diagram summarises the statistics used in this course.

EQUIPMENT

The equipment needed to carry out a statistical technique includes:

- paper
- a pencil
- a rubber/eraser
- a calculator – simple or statistical
- a computer software package such as Microsoft Excel
- set(s) of data – for example, with two variables (independent and dependent)
- a plotted graph – for example, a scatter graph of the two variables (pp. 62 and 63)
- the results from a statistical technique to compare with another technique, or to test the level of significance – for example, the Spearman rank correlation coefficient versus the Pearson product moment correlation coefficient
- critical value tables (head to the Digital Zone for more information on these).

PRESENTATION

As part of your learning, it is important that you complete the statistical techniques on paper, by hand, showing the full, detailed application of the statistical technique, including all stages in the calculation of the result (see the worked examples for each of the statistical techniques on pp. 40–53). The other methods illustrated are optional for use within the coursework.

Be methodical to ensure that no mistake is made in entering data or in your calculations and results.

Present your data, formulae, calculations and results in a clear and easy-to-understand manner.

You are expected to explain, in detail, the result(s) from the statistical technique(s) used within the context of the problem. This analysis of the result(s) is expected to refer to relevant and current geographical knowledge and understanding.

Within the context of the coursework (geographical study and geographical issue), you are free to use any method that produces a result. Techniques used within the coursework should be integrated into the context of that coursework and not be just an 'add-on' item.

Candidates who use appropriate and relevant statistical techniques within the context of their coursework are more likely to achieve higher marks. It is not the number of statistical techniques you include that is important, but their relevance and sophistication. You are expected to use more complex statistical techniques that show relationships, or differences, and that allow more detailed analyses.

The links to videos and online materials in this guide are for illustrative purposes and will support your learning. You are free to use other similar resources that you might identify during your research.

VIDEO LINK 

Watch the video on basic statistics at www.brightredbooks.net for a good overview.

ONLINE 

The link at www.brightredbooks.net will take you to a good, simple glossary for a wide range of statistical terms.

DON'T FORGET 

Don't allow your learning to get lost in a bundle of internet links.

VIDEO LINK 

Head to www.brightredbooks.net to find a series of videos on the A–Z of statistics.

ONLINE TEST 

Test yourself on the use of statistics at www.brightredbooks.net

ONLINE 

Check out the section 'What statistical test should I use?' at www.brightredbooks.net

HANDLING DIFFERENT TYPES OF DATA

There are four measurement scales (or types of data): nominal, ordinal, interval and ratio. These are simply ways of categorising different types of variables.

SAMPLING METHODS

In statistical analysis, sampling is a process in which a pre-determined number of observations are taken from a larger population. The sampling method used will depend on the type of analysis to be undertaken. We focus here on three simple sampling methods: random, stratified and regular/systematic. Refer to the guidance on p. 9

HYPOTHESIS TESTING

A hypothesis is a tentative statement about the relationship between two or more variables. It is a specific, testable prediction about what you expect to happen – for example, 'there is a significant relationship between altitude and soil fertility on a slope'.

A **null hypothesis** is the opposite statement – that is, there is no relationship between the variables. This is the statement that we test and try to disprove – for example, 'there is no significant relationship between altitude and soil fertility on a slope'.

We use the null hypothesis to prove whether there is a statistically significant relationship between variables. Our conclusion, after testing, will be either to accept or to reject the null hypothesis.

THINGS TO DO AND THINK ABOUT

Be aware of the potential for links that exist between a range of different techniques – for example, pebble analysis, scatter graphs, linear regression and correlation coefficients.

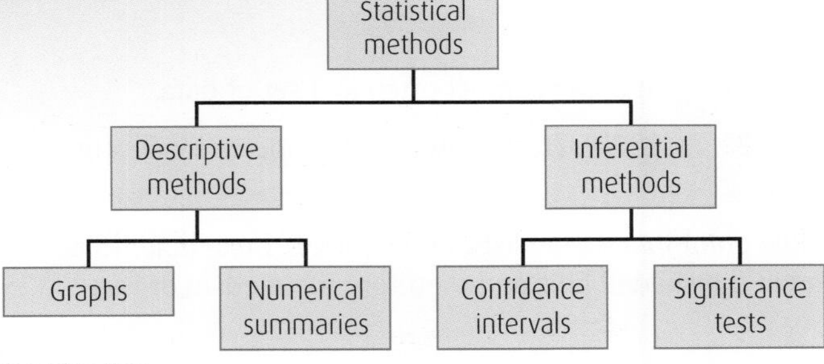

Decision tree.

As you work through the statistical techniques on pp. 38–53, think about the links that exist within the statistical techniques and between the other geographical techniques in this study guide:

- data-gathering techniques for physical geography (pp. 8–23)
- data-gathering techniques for human geography (pp. 24–37)
- graphical techniques (pp. 54–63)
- mapping techniques (pp. 64–81)
- coursework (geographical study and geographical issue) (pp. 82–89)
- the question paper (pp. 90–95).

VIDEO LINK

Watch the videos: (1) on how to remember the difference between nominal, ordinal, interval and ratio data at www.brightredbooks.net. This video has an excellent explanation and includes the different types of test that can be used; and (2) to understand and use the three types of sampling techniques. Note that in this example the sample is determined before gathering the data. Refer to the information about sampling on p. 8 and in the summary table.

You always need to use the most appropriate technique(s).

VIDEO LINK

Watch the video at www.brightredbooks.net, which gives a good, simple explanation of how to write different types of hypotheses and follow the link for detailed information on hypothesis testing, the null hypothesis and significance levels.

ONLINE

Use the link to the calculator at www.brightredbooks.net to determine the sample size required – for example, how many people you need to interview to obtain results that reflect the target population. The calculator will also allow you to determine the level of precision in an existing sample.

ONLINE

Learn more about data analysis using inferential statistics at www.brightredbooks.net

DESCRIPTIVE STATISTICS: MEASURES OF CENTRAL TENDENCY

Descriptive statistics are used to analyse and represent data that have already been collected. The techniques include frequency counts, ranges (high and low scores or values), the mode, median, mean, and standard deviation. Two important concepts in understanding descriptive statistics are:

- variables
- distribution.

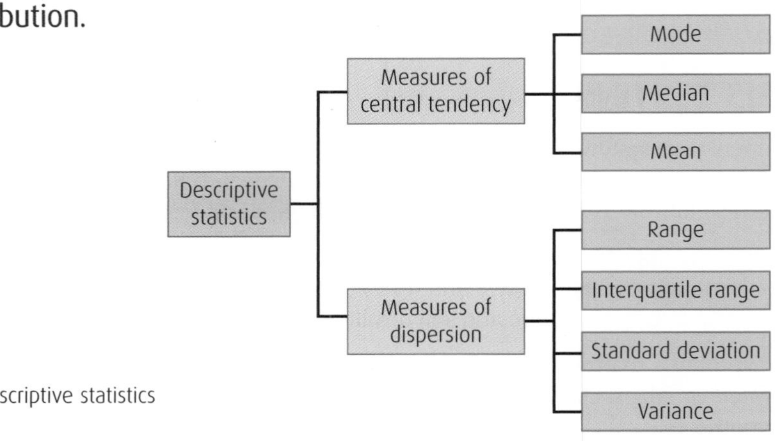

Descriptive statistics

PURPOSE

A measure of central tendency tells us the middle point in a set of data. The three most common measures of central tendency are the mean, median and mode.

METHODOLOGY

Mode: the mode is simply the number that appears most often in a set of data.

For example, in the set of data 21, 22, 21, 23, 19, 21, the number 21 appears most often, and therefore the mode is 21.

Median: the median is the middle point in a sorted list of numbers. For example, 15 is the middle point of the data set in the shaded box, and therefore the median of this data set is 15.

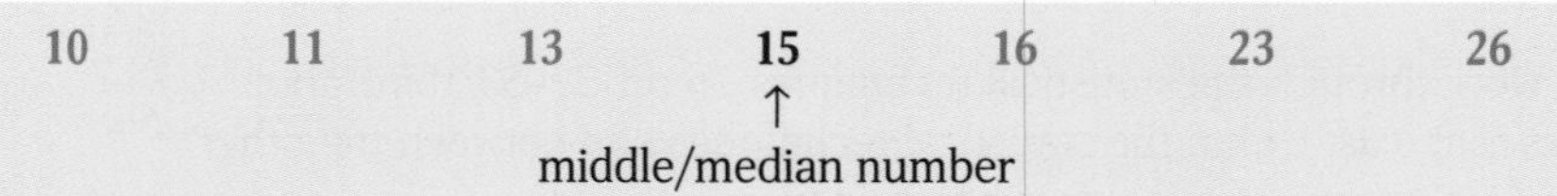

If there is an even number of items in a data set, then the median is the mean of the two middle numbers. To find the median value, first line the numbers up in order from the lowest to the highest.

For example, in the set of data 19, 20, 21, 22, 23, 24, the centre value or median lies between 21 and 22, and therefore the median value is the mean of these two values (21·5).

Mean: the mean is the most common measure of central tendency. It is calculated by adding up all the numbers in a data set and then dividing by the total number of items in the data set. This is also commonly known as the 'average'.

$$\text{Mean} = \frac{\text{the total (sum) of all the numbers in the data set}}{\text{the number of items in the data set}}$$

$$\frac{6+3+7+8}{3} = \frac{24}{3} = 8$$

contd

DON'T FORGET

Refer to the detailed information on pp. 38 and 39 for the equipment needed for the collection and presentation of statistics.

VIDEO LINK

Watch the video at www.brightredbooks.net on measures of central tendency for a short summary of the definitions of the mean, median and mode.

The mean is expressed as $\bar{x}$ (x-bar):

$$\bar{x} = \frac{\sum x}{n}$$

where n is the number of items in the data set, and the total (sum) of the numbers in the data set is expressed as $\sum x$. In statistics, the symbol $\sum$ (sigma) is used to denote 'the sum of'.

CONSIDERATIONS AND LIMITATIONS

Outliers: values that lie a long way outside the other values in the data set.

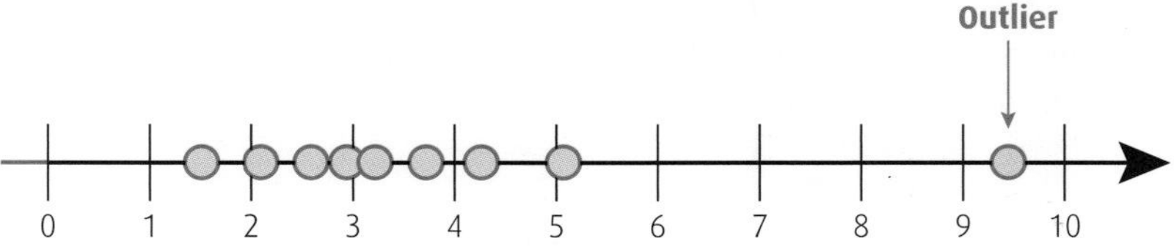

Example of an outlier.

What do we do with outliers? Can we just get rid of values we don't like?

When we remove outliers, we are changing the data set. It is no longer 'pure', so we must have a very good reason to get rid of the outliers. And when we do get rid of them, we should explain what we are doing and why.

Outliers have the largest effect on the mean and less effect on the median or mode.

Mode = 8·1mm
Median = 7·8mm
Mean = 7·96mm

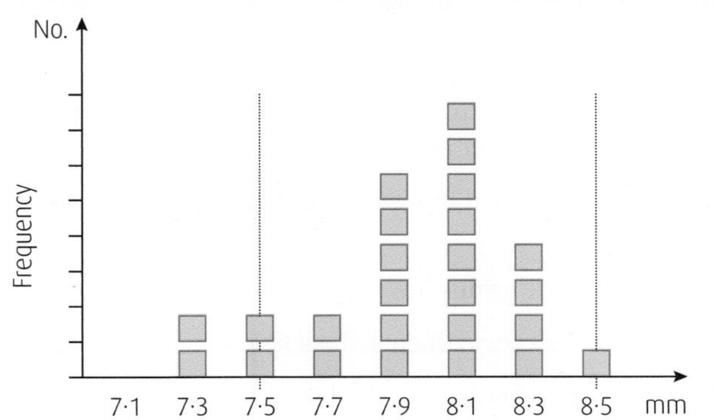

Descriptive statistics.

THINGS TO DO AND THINK ABOUT

Refer to the generic advice on pp. 38 and 39 and the following specific points.

Think about the possible links that measures of central tendency have with other geographical techniques in this study guide.

It is easy to carry out calculations with small data sets in your head, but you should use a calculator when working with large sets of data.

DON'T FORGET

Hint: calculate the median and mode when you have outliers.

ONLINE

Follow the link at www.brightredbooks.net to BBC Bitesize for some good, simple examples of measures of central tendency.

ONLINE

Use the links at www.brightredbooks.net for more on measures of central tendency and dispersion.

ONLINE

Check out the Glossary for this study guide at www.brightredbooks.net

ONLINE TEST

Head to www.brightredbooks.net to test yourself on measures of central tendency.

DESCRIPTIVE STATISTICS: MEASURES OF DISPERSION

PURPOSE

Measures of dispersion are important for describing the spread of data around a central value. Two distinct samples may have the same mean or median but may have completely different levels of spread, or vice versa. A correct description of a data set should include both of these characteristics. Several different methods can be used to measure the dispersion of a data set, each with its own advantages and disadvantages.

VIDEO LINK

Watch the video on measures of dispersion at www.brightredbooks.net

VIDEO LINK

Watch the video on how to find the range at www.brightredbooks.net. This video shows how to find the range for a given set of data. Remember to subtract the minimum value from the maximum value.

VIDEO LINK

Watch the video on how to compute the IQR at www.brightredbooks.net

ONLINE

See an example of calculating standard deviation at www.brightredbooks.net

VIDEO LINK

Watch the video on standard deviation at www.brightredbooks.net

METHODOLOGY

Range: the maximum minus the minimum value in a data set.

It is a crude measure of the variation (spread) of the data.

For example, in the maximum value in the data set 13, 15, 17, 19, 19, 19, 28, 30, 30, 32, 33, 34 is 34 and the minimum value is 13. Therefore the range is 34 – 13 = 21.

Interquartile range (IQR): a quartile is one of three points that divide a range of data or a population into four equal parts. The first quartile (also called the lower quartile, Q_1) is the number below which 25% of the data lies. The second quartile (the median) divides the range in the middle, and 50% of the data lies below it. The third quartile (also called the upper quartile, Q_3) is the number below which 75% of the data lies; 25% of the data lies above Q_3.

The IQR is the difference between the upper (Q_3) and lower (Q_1) quartiles and is expressed as:

IQR = upper quartile minus lower quartile (IQR = $Q_3 - Q_1$).

As a measure of the spread of data, the IQR is less sensitive to extreme outliers than the range.

Use the following formulas to calculate the IQR:

Upper quartile (Q_3)

$$Q_3 = \frac{3(n+1)}{4}$$

Lower quartile (Q_1)

$$Q_1 = \frac{(n+1)}{4}$$

where n = number of items in the data set.

For example, for the data set 3, 5, 5, 7, 8, 8, 9, 10, 13, 13, 14, 15, 16, 22, 23

$$Q_3 = \frac{3(15+1)}{4} = \frac{48}{4} = 12$$

$$Q_1 = \frac{16}{4} = 4$$

IQR = $Q_3 - Q_1$ = 12 – 4 = 8.

Standard deviation (S): this is a measure of the dispersion, or spread, of data around the mean. All the data in a sample is used. The formula is:

$$S = \sqrt{\frac{\Sigma(x-\bar{x})^2}{n-1}}$$

where S = standard deviation, x = individual data values, $\bar{x}$ = mean, n = number of items in the data set and Σ (sigma) = the 'sum of'.

CONSIDERATIONS AND LIMITATIONS

Normal distribution: a normal distribution occurs in a data set in which most values cluster in the middle of the range and the rest taper off symmetrically towards either extreme.

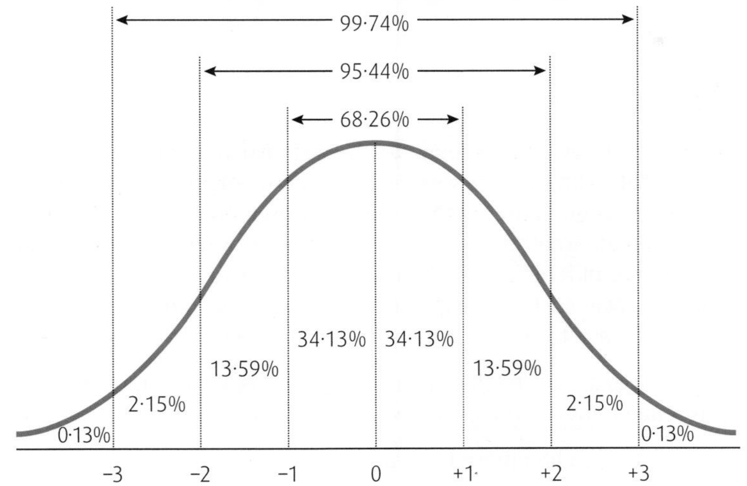

Example of a normal distribution.

Standard error of the mean (SE): this is a measure of the accuracy of the sample mean as an estimate of the population mean.

The formula is:

$SE_{\bar{x}} = \frac{S}{\sqrt{n}}$

where $SE_{\bar{x}}$ = standard error of the mean, S = standard deviation and n = number of items in the data set.

Therefore, for the data set (1, 2, 3, 4 and 5), the calculation is:

$SE_{\bar{x}} = \frac{1.41}{\sqrt{5}} = 0{\cdot}63.$

Coefficient of variation (CV): this is the ratio of the standard deviation to the mean. The higher the CV, the greater the level of dispersion around the mean. It is generally expressed as a percentage. The CV does not have units, and it allows a comparison to be made between distributions of values with scales of measurement that are not comparable.

The formula is:

$CV = \frac{S}{\bar{x}} \times 100.$

Therefore, for the data set (1, 2, 3, 4 and 5), the calculation would be:

$CV = \frac{1{\cdot}41}{3} = 0{\cdot}47 \times 100 = 47.$

THINGS TO DO AND THINK ABOUT

Refer to the generic advice on pp. 38 and 39 and the following specific points.

Think about the possible links that measures of dispersion have with other geographical techniques in this study guide.

It is easy to carry out calculations with small data sets in your head, but use a calculator when working with large sets of data.

DON'T FORGET

Standard deviation is the most robust measure of variability because it takes into account a measure of how every value in the data set varies from the mean.

ONLINE

For information about the advantages and disadvantages of measures of dispersion, including additional worked examples, read the article at www.brightredbooks.net

ONLINE

Follow the link at www.brightredbooks.net for more on dispersion statistics.

ONLINE

Use the links at www.brightredbooks.net to find out more on measures of central tendency and dispersion.

VIDEO LINK

Watch the video on the standard error of the mean at www.brightredbooks.net

VIDEO LINK

To find out more about the coefficient of variation, watch the video at www.brightredbooks.net

ONLINE TEST

Head to www.brightredbooks.net to test yourself on measures of dispersion.

INFERENTIAL STATISTICS: CHI-SQUARED ANALYSIS

DON'T FORGET 

Refer to the detailed information on pp. 38 and 39 for the equipment needed for the collection and presentation of statistics.

ONLINE 

View the video at www.brightredbooks.net for further information on the chi-squared test.

VIDEO LINK 

Check out the clip 'How to perform a chi-squared test by hand' at www.brightredbooks.net

VIDEO LINK 

View the practical example of using a chi-squared test on data resulting from an urban field-studies exercise at www.brightredbooks.net

ONLINE 

Use the practical example of the seashore (types of seaweed) at www.brightredbooks.net as a further guide.

PURPOSE

The chi-squared test (also written as the χ^2 test) is a statistical test commonly used to compare observed data with the data we would expect to obtain according to a specific hypothesis – that is, how good the fit is between the observed data and the expected data. It can be used to determine whether there are differences between the observed and expected data and whether these differences are the result of chance or whether they are due to factors that can be explained. It can help you, the investigator, to decide how much deviation can occur before you have to conclude that something other than chance is at work.

The chi-squared test is always testing the null hypothesis, which states that there is no significant difference between the expected and observed results.

The requirements for the chi-squared test are:

- quantitative data
- one or more categories of data
- independent observations
- an adequate sample size (at least ten)
- a simple, random sample
- data in frequency form
- all observations must be used.

The formula for working out the value of chi-squared (χ^2) is: $\chi^2 = \sum\frac{(O - E)^2}{E}$

where O is the observed data and E is the expected data.

The result of the chi-squared test has to be checked against the relevant significance tables. It is necessary to calculate the degree of freedom (df), which equals (n – 1), where n is the number of categories.

METHODOLOGY

The chi-squared test can be calculated using several different methods.

1. By hand.

Example:

We expect to find equal numbers of yellow, red, green, blue and white balls in a bag of 100 coloured balls.

However, on checking the contents of the bag, the observed numbers are 10 yellow, 15 red, 30 green, 20 blue and 25 white balls.

We can use the chi-squared test to determine whether the observed frequencies differ significantly from the expected frequencies.

In this instance, the null hypothesis states that there is no significant difference between the expected and observed frequencies. This what we want to test.

The steps in using the chi-squared test can be summarised as follows:

- construct a table
- write the observed frequencies in row O (observed)
- calculate the expected frequencies and write them in row E (expected)

	YELLOW	RED	GREEN	BLUE	WHITE	
O	10	15	30	20	25	
E	20	20	20	20	20	
$(O - E)$	−10	−5	10	0	5	
$(O - E)^2$	100	25	100	0	25	
$\frac{(O - E)^2}{E}$	5	1·25	5	0	1·25	$\sum\frac{(O - E)^2}{E}$ = 12·5
						χ^2 = 12·5

contd

- insert the values for $(O - E)$
- insert the values for $(O - E)^2$
- use the formula to find the value of chi-squared (χ^2)
- work out the degree of freedom (df) using $(n - 1)$, in this case $(5 - 1 = 4)$
- consult the critical table value for the chi-squared test (refer to the chi-squared critical values on the Digital Zone)
- begin by finding the calculated degree of freedom along the left-hand side of the table, then run your fingers across this row until you reach the pre-determined level of significance (0·05) in the column heading at the top of the table.

The table value for chi-squared in the correct box for four degrees of freedom and a level of significance of $P = 0{\cdot}05$ is 9·49.
If your chi-squared value is equal to or greater than the table value, then you reject the null hypothesis, which means that the differences in your data are not due to chance alone.
We therefore reject the null hypothesis in this instance.

It is worth considering that this statistical test tells you nothing about the outside influences on the contents of the bag. All we have proved is that our observed frequencies are different from the expected frequencies. You could criticise this approach by pointing out that we assumed that the expected value would be the same.

Perhaps, in any evaluation of the result, we need to consider:

- Was the sample used too small?
- Would another statistical test have been more suitable in this instance?
- Should we use another statistical test to confirm our result?

2. Using Microsoft Excel or other spreadsheet software
3. Using an online calculator for the chi-squared test

   As with all statistical tests, you must decide whether there is sufficient evidence to accept, or reject, the null hypothesis. Relate the result to the scale of critical values. Remember that we have to be 95% confident that this result is not a statistical fluke. We therefore use the 0·05 level of significance.

CONSIDERATIONS AND LIMITATIONS

ADVANTAGES	DISADVANTAGES
can test associations between variables is useful in measuring the differences between what is observed and expected useful when the expected distribution of the data is unknown useful when data can be grouped into classes the chi-squared value can be compared with significance tables to confirm whether any deviation from random in the observed data is a chance effect or has statistical significance	cannot use percentages data must be in the form of frequencies data must have precise numerical values and be organised into categories or groups categories of two are not good to compare the number of observations must be more than 20 the expected frequency in any one cell must be more than 5 the test becomes invalid if any of the expected values are below 5 fairly complicated to get right – difficult formula

THINGS TO DO AND THINK ABOUT

Refer to the generic advice on pp. 38 and 39 and the following specific points.

Think about the possible links that the chi-squared test has with other geographical techniques in this study guide.

ONLINE

Use the link at www.brightredbooks.net to access the chi-squared critical values table.

VIDEO LINK

Head to www.brightredbooks.net to see the clips on the chi-squared test in Microsoft Excel.

ONLINE

Use any of the websites linked from www.brightredbooks.net to calculate a chi-squared test

DON'T FORGET

The value of chi-squared should not be calculated if the expected value in any category is less than 5.

ONLINE TEST

Head to www.brightredbooks.net to test yourself on the chi-squared test.

ONLINE

Head to www.brightredbooks.net for three examples to practise or test yourself on the chi-squared test.

INFERENTIAL STATISTICS: SPEARMAN RANK CORRELATION COEFFICIENT (SRCC)

DON'T FORGET

Refer to the detailed information on pp. 38 and 39 for the equipment needed for the collection and presentation of statistics.

Charles Spearman (1863–1945), British psychologist and pioneer of IQ theory.

DON'T FORGET

This test uses ranked ordinal data and is a good guide to the presence of a relationship.

ONLINE

Use any of the websites at www.brightredbooks.net to calculate the SRCC.

ONLINE

Follow the link at www.brightredbooks.net for more detail.

VIDEO LINK

Watch the video at www.brightredbooks.net to see how to calculate the SRCC.

PURPOSE

The Spearman rank correlation coefficient (SRCC) measures the strength and direction of a relationship between two variables and ranges from −1 to 1. As a statistical technique, it is used to accept, or reject, a null hypothesis – for example, 'the width of a river does not progressively increase further downstream'.

There are two methods of calculating the SRCC depending on whether or not the data has tied ranks. Tied ranks occur when you have identical values in a data set and you do not know which value should be ranked first. In this case, you need to take the average of the values and assign the tied rank to each.

The formula for working out the SRCC (r_s) when there is no tied rank is:

$$r_S = 1 - \frac{6\Sigma d^2}{n^3 - n} \text{ or } \rho = 1 - \frac{6\Sigma d_i^2}{n(n^2 - 1)}$$

The formula to use when there are tied ranks is:

$$\rho = \frac{\Sigma_i(x_i - \bar{x})(y_i - \bar{y})}{\sqrt{\Sigma_i(x_i - \bar{x})^2\Sigma_i(y_i - \bar{y})^2}}$$

where r_s or ρ = SRCC, Σ = 'sum of', d or d_i = difference in paired ranks, n = number of pairs of data, x or y = individual values, $\bar{x}$ or $\bar{y}$ = mean of the values and i = paired scores.

METHODOLOGY

The SRCC can be calculated by several different methods.

1. By hand
   The test is not reliable with less than ten pairs, as in our example, and becomes arithmetically difficult with more than 30 pairs. The following example is to illustrate the process

Example:

The steps in calculating the SRCC may be summarised as follows:

- construct a table
- write in the values for the variables – data set 1
- write in the values for the variables – data set 2
- draw a scatter graph (p. 62) to see whether there is a correlation between the two sets of variables
- establish the null hypothesis – 'there is no relationship between data set 1 and data set 2'
- rank data set 1 under rank 1 – lowest to highest
- rank data set 2 under rank 2 – lowest to highest
- calculate the difference between the two numbers in the pair of ranks and insert into column *d*
- calculate the square of column d and insert into column d^2
- work out the sum of d^2 (Σd^2).

Data set 1	Data set 2	Rank 1	Rank 2	d	d^2
7	15	3	5	2	4
5	8	2	3	1	1
3	9	1	4	3	9
10	5	4	2	2	4
12	2	5	1	4	16
					$\Sigma d^2 = 34$

Now choose the correct formula: non-tied or tied.
In this example, we use the non-tied formula:

$$r_s = 1 - \frac{6\Sigma d^2}{(n^3 - n)}$$

$$r_s = 1 - \frac{(6 \times 34)}{(125 - 5)} = \frac{204}{120} = 1 - 1{\cdot}7 = -0{\cdot}70.$$

contd

Now interpret the result.

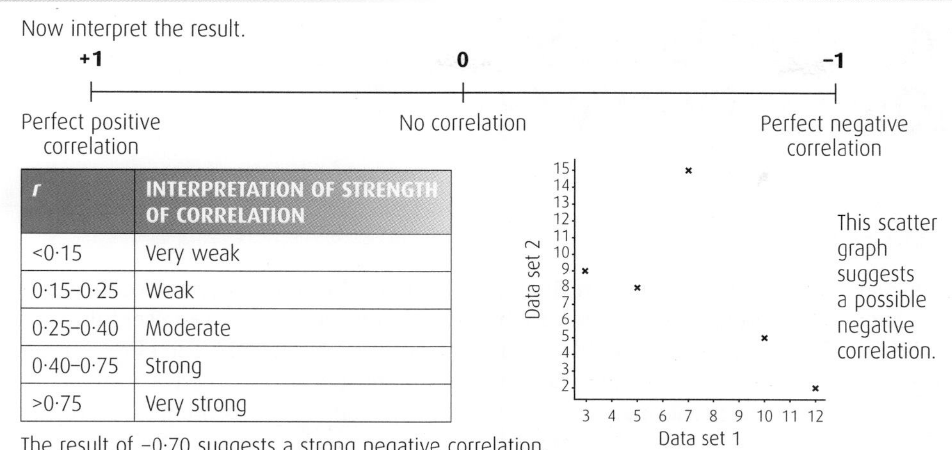

r	INTERPRETATION OF STRENGTH OF CORRELATION
<0·15	Very weak
0·15–0·25	Weak
0·25–0·40	Moderate
0·40–0·75	Strong
>0·75	Very strong

The result of −0·70 suggests a strong negative correlation.

A further technique is now required to test the significance of the relationship.

- Work out the degree of freedom (df) using *n*. In this case, we have five pairs, so *n* = 5.
- Look at the critical table value for the SRCC on the Digital Zone.
- Begin by finding the degree of freedom along the left-hand side of the table. Run your fingers across the correct row until you reach the pre-determined level of significance (0·05) in the column heading at the top of the table.

The table value for SRCC in the correct box for five degrees of freedom and the *P* = 0·05 level of significance is 0·900.

If your SRCC is equal to, or greater than, the table value, then you reject the null hypothesis. This means that the differences in your data are not due to chance alone.

In this instance, however, we must accept the null hypothesis because our value of −0·70 is less than the table value of 0·90. This confirms, with statistical significance, what we predicted from the scatter graph plot and the value of the SRCC.

However, it is worth considering that this statistical test does not imply any causal relationship between the data sets (variables) – that is, whether a change in one variable leads to a change in the other variable.

2. Using Microsoft Excel or spreadsheet software
3. Online calculators

CONSIDERATIONS AND LIMITATIONS

In any evaluation of the result we need to consider:

- Was the sample used, as in this case, too small, so we need to gather more data?
- Did we perform a lot of calculations to determine whether we had insufficient data, which should have been realised earlier from the scatter graph?
- Use Microsoft Excel, or an online calculator, to check and confirm the result.
- Would another statistical test been more suitable in this instance?
- Should we use another statistical test to confirm our result, such as the Pearson product moment correlation coefficient (pp. 48 and 49)?

THINGS TO DO AND THINK ABOUT

Refer to the generic advice on pp. 38 and 39 and the following specific points.

Think about the possible links that the SRCC has with other geographical techniques in this study guide.

The SRCC does not use absolute data values. The ranking of the data reduces the impact of extreme values. Consequently, its accuracy is less than that of the Pearson product moment correlation (pp. 48 and 49).

Head to the Digital Zone for more on the SRCC.

ONLINE

Check out the practical example of using the SRCC based on resources from the Barcelona Field Studies Centre at www.brightredbooks.net and read the document in full to appreciate the limitations of the SRCC.

VIDEO LINK

Watch the video or follow the link at www.brightredbooks.net to see how to use Microsoft Excel to calculate the SRCC.

ONLINE

Use the critical values table at www.brightredbooks.net to test the level of significance.

ONLINE

For more on interpreting the results of a SRCC test, follow the link at www.brightredbooks.net

ONLINE TEST

Head to www.brightredbooks.net to test yourself on the SRCC.

VIDEO LINK

Check out the clip comparing the use of the Pearson product moment correlation coefficient and the SRCC at www.brightredbooks.net

INFERENTIAL STATISTICS: PEARSON PRODUCT MOMENT CORRELATION COEFFICIENT (PPMCC)

DON'T FORGET

Refer to the detailed information on pp. 38 and 39 for the equipment needed for the collection and presentation of statistics.

ONLINE

The link at www.brightredbooks.net gives more details of the PPMCC.

VIDEO LINK

The videos at www.brightredbooks.net show how to calculate the PPMCC by hand and using Microsoft Excel.

ONLINE TEST

Head to www.brightredbooks.net to test yourself on the PPMCC.

ONLINE

Head to www.brightredbooks.net to see the full steps of the calculation.

DON'T FORGET

Always remember to check the level of significance.

PURPOSE

The Pearson product moment correlation coefficient (PPMCC) is a measure of the strength of a linear relationship between two variables. Two letters are used to represent the PPMCC: a Greek rho (ρ) for a population and the letter r for a sample. The PPMCC ranges from −1 to 1, with values of −1 representing the strongest possible negative correlation, 1 representing the strongest possible positive correlation and 0 representing no correlation. As a statistical technique, it is used to accept or reject a null hypothesis – for example, 'crime rates do not decrease the further you are from the central business district'.

The requirements for using the PPMCC are:

- the scale of measurement should be an interval or ratio
- the variables should be approximately normally distributed
- the association should be linear
- there should be no outlier in the data.

The formula for working out the PPMCC (r) is:

$$r = \frac{\sum_i (x - \bar{x})(y - \bar{y})}{\sqrt{\sum_i (x - \bar{x})^2 \sum_i (y - \bar{y})^2}}$$

where r or ρ = the PPMCC, $\sum$ = 'sum of', x or y = individual values, $\bar{x}$ or $\bar{y}$ = mean of the values and $\sqrt{}$ = square root.

METHODOLOGY

The PPMCC can be calculated using several different methods.

1. By hand

Example:

A student gathers data at 12 points along a river by measuring the discharge of the river and the size of the bedload at each point (pp. 20 and 21). Through wider reading, the student is aware that the discharge tends to increase downstream, whereas the bedload size generally decreases. The student expects to see a negative relationship between the two variables and proposed the null hypothesis 'there is no relationship between discharge and bedload size'.

The student constructed a scatter graph (p. 62) to illustrate the existence of a negative relationship and added a line of best fit.

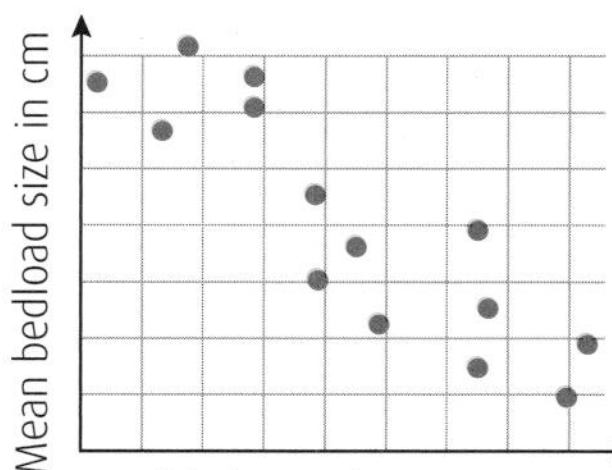

This scatter graph suggests a negative correlation.

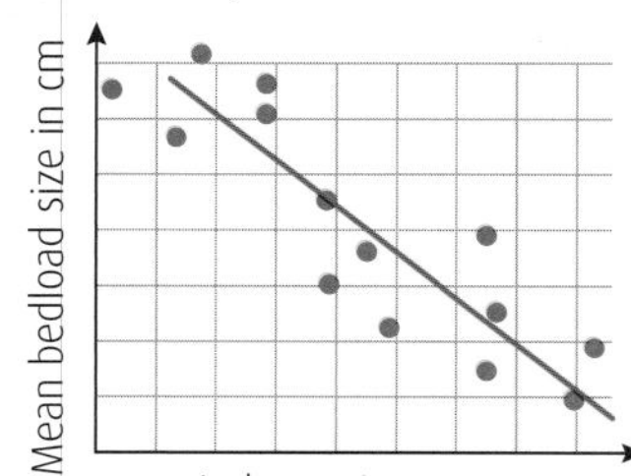

Line of best fit on the scatter graph.

The student then decides to test the strength of the relationship using the Pearson product moment correlation coefficient.

This means we now have all the figures to complete the formula as follows:

$$r = \frac{\sum(x - \bar{x})(y - \bar{y})}{\sqrt{\sum(x - \bar{x})^2 \sum(y - \bar{y})^2}}$$

$$r = -\frac{13{\cdot}61}{\sqrt{(11{\cdot}11)(19{\cdot}51)}} = \frac{13{\cdot}61}{\sqrt{216{\cdot}76}} = \frac{13{\cdot}61}{14{\cdot}72} = -0{\cdot}92 \text{ (to 2 significant figures).}$$

The negative value for r indicates a strong negative correlation.

contd

A further technique is now required to test the significance of the relationship:

- Work out the degrees of freedom using (n – 1). In this case, it would be (12 – 1) = 11.
- Look up the critical table value for the PPMCC on the Digital Zone.
- Find the calculated degree of freedom along the left-hand side of the table and then run your fingers across the correct row until you reach the pre-determined level of significance (0·05) in the column heading on the top of the table.

The table value for the PPMCC in the correct box for 11 degrees of freedom at the P = 0·05 level of significance is 0·476.

If your PPMCC is equal to or greater than the table value, then you reject the null hypothesis, and the differences in your data are not due to chance alone.

In this instance, we can reject the null hypothesis, as our value of −0·92 exceeds the critical value of 0·476 at the 0·05 level of significance. In fact, it also exceeds the 0·01 level of significance. We therefore can reject the null hypothesis at the 99% level of confidence. This confirms, with statistical significance, what may have been predicted from the scatter-graph plot and field observations.

It is worth considering that this statistical test does not imply any causal relationship between the variables – that is, a change in one variable leads to a change in the other.

Perhaps in any evaluation of the result we need to consider:

- Was the sample used too small – do we need to gather more data?
- Would another statistical test have been more suitable to use in this instance?
- Use Microsoft Excel, or an online calculator, to check and confirm the result.
- Should we use another statistical test to confirm our result – for example, the SRCC (pp. 46 and 47) and/or linear regression (pp. 50 and 51)?

2. Using Microsoft Excel

3. Online calculators

CONSIDERATIONS AND LIMITATIONS

Although widely used, this statistical test has its limitations:

- it assumes a linear relationship between the variables even if this does not exist
- a high degree of correlation does not necessarily mean a close causal relationship between the variables
- it is tedious to calculate
- it is unduly affected by the values of extreme items.

For example, for values for x = 1, 2, 3, 4, 5 and values of y = 5, 4, 3, 2, 1, the PPMCC = 0.

However, if we have x = 1, 2, 3, 4, 5, 100 and y = 5, 4, 3, 2, 1, 120, then the PPMCC = +0·99.

The addition of one large value to each data set has boosted the correlation from zero to +0·99.

THINGS TO DO AND THINK ABOUT

Refer to the generic advice for the use of statistics on pp. 38 and 39 and the following specific points.

Think about the possible links that the PPMCC has with other geographical techniques in this study guide.

Head to the Digital Zone for more on the PPMCC.

Consider using linear regression analysis (pp. 50 and 51).

ONLINE

Head to www.brightredbooks.net for the critical values table.

VIDEO LINK

Watch the video on hypothesis testing with the PPMCC at www.brightredbooks.net

DON'T FORGET

This technique attempts to draw a line of best fit through the data for two variables.

ONLINE

Check out the Microsoft Excel version of this example at www.brightredbooks.net

ONLINE

Use any of the websites at www.brightredbooks.net to calculate a PPMCC.

ONLINE

Practise some online questions on the PPMCC at www.brightredbooks.net

VIDEO LINK

Watch the clip at www.brightredbooks.net for more on the PPMCC.

VIDEO LINK

For an extra tutorial on the PPMCC, watch the clip at www.brightredbooks.net

INFERENTIAL STATISTICS: LINEAR REGRESSION ANALYSIS

DON'T FORGET

Refer to the detailed information on pp. 38 and 39 for the equipment needed for the collection and presentation of statistics.

PURPOSE

This statistical technique is the most commonly used method of predictive analysis to determine the linear relationship between one dependent variable and one independent variable. The regression equation allows us to mathematically calculate and plot the best-fit line on a scatter graph with a higher degree of certainty than a more subjective plotting by eye.

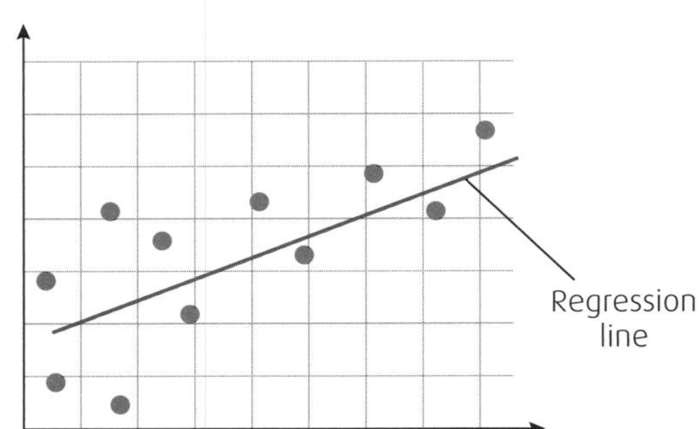

The formula for linear regression can be shown in a number of different ways. Here, we will use:

$y = a + bx$

where x is the independent variable, y is the dependent variable, b is the slope/gradient of the regression line and a is the intercept point where the best-fit line crosses the y-axis (the value of y when $x = 0$).

To conduct a regression analysis, we need to solve for b and a.

The computations are:
Slope (b) of regression line:

$b = r\frac{S_y}{S_x}$

where r = correlation coefficient, S_y = standard deviation of y, S_x = standard deviation of x (refer to the section on standard deviation on pp. 42 and 43) and y = intercept (a) of the regression line:

$a = \bar{y} - b\bar{x}$

where $\bar{x}$ = mean of x values, $\bar{y}$ = mean of y values and b = slope of regression.

VIDEO LINK

The video on the Digital Zone explains a simple linear regression, the coefficient of determination and correlation coefficient.

ONLINE

As a follow-up to the video, see the worked example for physical geography at www.brightredbooks.net

VIDEO LINK

Check out the clip at www.brightredbooks.net

ONLINE TEST

Head to www.brightredbooks.net to test yourself on linear regression analysis.

METHODOLOGY

The linear regression line can be calculated using several different methods. The links are to videos showing how to carry out a linear regression analysis.

1. By hand

Example:

This example assumes you have watched the videos and you have successfully learned how to calculate a Pearson product moment correlation coefficient.

In this worked example, we use and refer to the data, scatter graph, table of data and the Pearson product moment correlation coefficient result from pp. 48 and 49 – you should revise this information on the Pearson product moment correlation coefficient before proceeding.

Summary of the data table from pp. 48 and 49.

Sample points	Discharge (m^3/s) (x)	Mean bedload size (cm) (y)	$(x - \bar{x})$	$(y - \bar{y})$	$(x - \bar{x})(y - \bar{y})$	$(x - \bar{x})^2$	$(y - \bar{y})^2$
	$\bar{x}$ = 1·30	$\bar{y}$ = 2·36			Σ = −13·61	Σ = 11·11	Σ = 19·51
Pearson product moment correlation coefficient (r) = −0·92 (remember this is a negative value)							

contd

The following table outlines the steps to calculate the linear regression:

Linear regression formula $y = a + bx$		
Step 1: calculate slope (b) $b = r\frac{S_y}{S_x}$ To do this, we need to calculate S_x and S_y $= -0{\cdot}92\ \frac{1{\cdot}331}{1{\cdot}004} = -1.22$ $\mathbf{b = 1{\cdot}219}$	S_x = standard deviation of x $S = \frac{\sqrt{\Sigma(x - \bar{x})^2}}{(n - 1)}$ n = number in sample $S = \frac{\sqrt{11{\cdot}11}}{11} = \sqrt{1{\cdot}01} = 1{\cdot}00$	S_y = standard deviation of y $S = \frac{\sqrt{\Sigma(y - \bar{y})^2}}{(n - 1)}$ n = number in sample $S = \frac{\sqrt{19{\cdot}51}}{11} = \sqrt{1{\cdot}77} = 1{\cdot}33$
Step 2: Calculate the y-intercept (a) $a = \bar{y} - b\bar{x}$ $a = 2{\cdot}36 - (-1{\cdot}22 \times 1{\cdot}30) = 2{\cdot}36 - (-1{\cdot}59) = 3{\cdot}95$ $\mathbf{a = 3{\cdot}95}$ $(x - \bar{x})\ (y - \bar{y})$		
Step 3: Calculate the linear regression analysis using the formula: $\mathbf{y = a + bx}$ $y = 3{\cdot}95 + (-1{\cdot}22 \times x)$ From this, we can work out a value for y from a given value of x. If $x = 2{\cdot}20$, then $y = 3{\cdot}95 + (-1{\cdot}22 \times 2{\cdot}20) =$ **1·27**. This tells us that for an x value of 2·20, the y value is 1·27. You can also use Microsoft Excel or an online calculator to check the result, remembering that there might be slight numerical differences.		

2. Using Microsoft Excel
3. Using an online regression line calculator

ONLINE

Use any of the websites linked from www.brightredbooks.net to carry out a simple linear regression analysis.

VIDEO LINK

Head to www.brightredbooks.net to see the clips on linear regression analysis in Microsoft Excel.

ONLINE

Head to www.brightredbooks.net to download an example Microsoft Excel calculation and an example using an online calculator.

CONSIDERATIONS AND LIMITATIONS

Regression analysis has three uses:

- to identify the strength of the effect that the independent variable(s) has/have on a dependent variable
- to understand how much the dependent variable will change when we change the independent variable
- to predicts trends and future values.

Regression is based on several assumptions, which you can find out more about on the Digital Zone.

ONLINE

Head to www.brightredbooks.net for a link that explains, for background information for the exam, the limitations to linear regression analysis.

THINGS TO DO AND THINK ABOUT

Refer to the generic advice on pp. 38 and 39 and the following specific points.

Think about the possible links that linear regression analysis has with other geographical techniques in this study guide – for example, pebble analysis, scatter graphs and correlation coefficients.

How do you interpret your results within the context of the problem? Watch the videos at www.brightredbooks.net

DON'T FORGET

If the result feels or looks wrong when checked against the scatter graph, then check your calculations.

INFERENTIAL STATISTICS: NEAREST-NEIGHBOUR ANALYSIS

ONLINE 

View the Microsoft PowerPoint presentation at www.brightredbooks.net for further information.

PURPOSE

Nearest-neighbour analysis is a technique used to measure distributions according to whether they are clustered, random or regular. This technique can be used with any feature that can be regarded as being located at a specific point, such as settlements, shops, factories and trees. Using this technique, you can calculate the nearest-neighbour index, providing a level of statistical meaning to the terms clustered, random and regular.

The formula for working out the nearest-neighbour index (R_n) is:

$$R_n = 2\bar{d}\frac{\sqrt{n}}{a}$$

where R_n = nearest-neighbour index, $\bar{d}$ = the mean observed nearest-neighbour distance, n = the total number of points and a = the total area.

The nearest-neighbour formula will produce a result between 0 and 2·15.

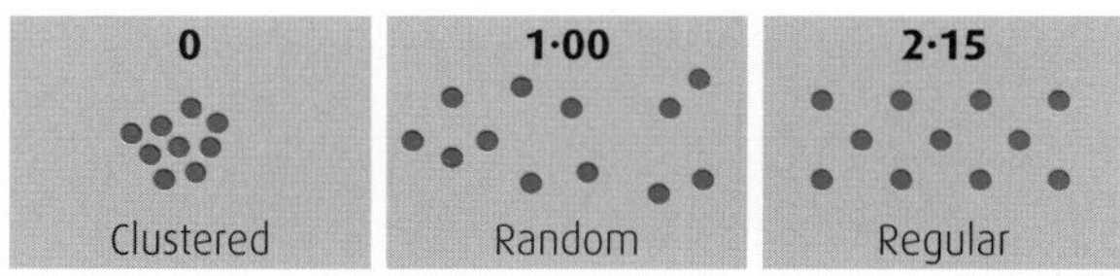

(a) R_n = 0. All the dots are close to the same point.
(b) R_n = 1·0. There is no pattern.
(c) R_n = 2·15. There is a perfectly uniform pattern, where each dot is equidistant from its neighbours.

METHODOLOGY

Define the area under investigation and calculate its area (e.g. 29·6 km^2). Draw an accurate base map of the study area and then plot each point and assign it a number. From a visual inspection of the map, decide whether the points are clustered or dispersed.

State a null hypothesis based on your visual inspection – for example, 'The settlements in the defined area have a dispersed distribution'.

Construct and complete the following table, including all the points. Remember to use the same units of measurement – for example, metres or kilometres.

POINT NUMBER	NEAREST-NEIGHBOUR NUMBER	DISTANCE BETWEEN THE TWO POINTS (KM) (D)
1	3	6
2	6	8
3	8	3
4	7	2
5	3	5
6	2	2
7	4	4
8	7	3
		Total (ΣD) = 33

Add up all the distances d (ΣD) and divide by the number of points (n) to calculate the mean of the distances:

$$\bar{d} = \frac{33}{8} = 4{\cdot}13$$

contd

Now calculate the formula using the data:

$R_n = 2\bar{d}\left(\frac{\sqrt{n}}{a}\right) = (2 \times 4{\cdot}13)\left(\frac{\sqrt{8}}{29{\cdot}6}\right) = 8{\cdot}26 \times \left(\frac{2{\cdot}83}{29{\cdot}6}\right) = 8{\cdot}26 \times 0{\cdot}0956 = 0{\cdot}79$ (to 2 significant figures).

A value of 0·79 suggests that the points (settlements) are close to a clustered distribution.

As with all statistical tests, you must decide whether there is sufficient evidence to accept or reject the null hypothesis.

Relate the result to the scale of critical values (see Digital Zone). Remember that we have to be 95% confident that this result is not a statistical fluke. We therefore use the 0·05 level of significance. Use the number in the sample (n) to reject the null hypothesis. The critical values for clustering and dispersion are different. Make sure you consult the correct values in the table.

A value less than 0·696 is considered to indicate significant clustering at $P = 0{\cdot}05$. Similarly, a value greater than 1·304 indicates significant dispersal at $P = 0{\cdot}05$.

We can therefore reject the null hypothesis.

DON'T FORGET

The interquartile method may be a better option in some instances (pp. 42 and 43).

ONLINE TEST

Head to www.brightredbooks.net to test yourself on nearest-neighbour analysis.

CONSIDERATIONS AND LIMITATIONS

Ensure the scale of the map and the scale used to measure the area are the same. Area boundaries are often very subjective.

If the nearest-neighbour index is used to compare a feature in two or more areas, then these must be of similar size. This analysis is not very precise where there is more than one cluster. No account is taken of the influence of the physical landscape on the location of features, which can distort the result.

Calculation of the distribution of a tree species.

THINGS TO DO AND THINK ABOUT

Refer to the generic advice on pp. 38 and 39 and the following specific points.

Think about the possible links that nearest-neighbour analysis has with other geographical techniques in this study guide.

How to calculate a z-test? Follow the links and online calculator at www.brightredbooks.net

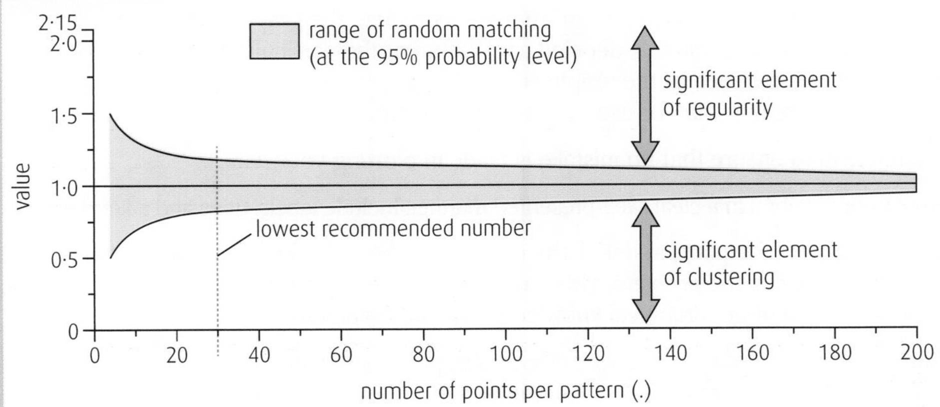

Interpretation of R_n statistic: significant values.

ONLINE

Head to www.brightredbooks.net to see two examples that you could use to practise or to test yourself.

ONLINE

Check out the PDF on nearest-neighbour analysis at www.brightredbooks.net

DON'T FORGET

Be methodical to ensure that no mistake is made in entering data or in your calculations and outputs.

GRAPHS

GENERAL ADVICE ON THE USE OF GRAPHS

PURPOSE

The graphical techniques explained on pp. 54–63 are those you are expected to know and understand for the examination. Within the context of the unit on geographical skills and the coursework (the geographical study and geographical issue), you are free to use any appropriate and relevant graphical technique.

A graph is a visual representation of a relationship between, but not restricted to, two variables. A graph generally takes the form of a one- or two-dimensional figure, such as a scatter graph. Although three-dimensional graphs are available, they are often considered to be too complex to understand easily, so should only be used when they actually add something to the understanding of the context.

A graph commonly, but not always, consists of two axes called the *x*-axis (horizontal) and *y*-axis (vertical). Each axis corresponds to one variable. The axes are labelled with different names, such as '*Size of …*' and '*Quantity of …*'.

Types of graphs:

- line graphs – simple, comparative, compound and divergent
- bar graphs – simple, comparative, compound and divergent
- scatter graphs – with the best-fit line
- pie charts and proportional divided circles
- triangular graphs
- kite and radial diagrams
- logarithmic graphs
- dispersion diagrams.

VIDEO LINK

Watch the videos on how to draw a wide range of graphs at www.brightredbooks.net

EQUIPMENT

The equipment needed to carry out a graphical technique includes:

- paper, a pencil and an eraser
- a calculator
- a computer with Microsoft Excel or a similar software package
- set(s) of data with two variables – independent and dependent
- graph paper
- map/diagram.

DON'T FORGET 

Don't allow your learning to get lost in a bundle of internet links.

PRESENTATION

As part of your learning, it is important that you complete the graphical techniques on paper by hand, showing the full, detailed application of the particular technique (see the worked examples for each of the graphical techniques on pp. 56–63). The other methods described here are optional for use within the coursework.

Be methodical to ensure that no mistake is made in plotting your data.

Present your graph(s) in a clear, well-presented manner. Include labels, titles and a key/legend.

You are expected to explain, in detail, the result(s) of the graphical technique(s) used within the context of the problem. This analysis of the result(s) is expected to refer to relevant and current geographical knowledge and understanding.

Within the context of the coursework (the geographical study and geographical issue), you are free to use any graphical technique or method of construction.

DON'T FORGET 

Knowing how to convey information graphically is important in presenting data.

contd

Candidates who use appropriate and relevant graphical techniques within the context of their coursework are more likely to achieve higher marks. It is not about the number of graphs you include, but their relevance and sophistication – for example, a single-line graph is less sophisticated than a multiple-line graph. You are expected to use more complex graphs showing relationships or differences that allow more detailed analyses.

The links to videos and online materials in this guide are for illustrative purposes and will help to support your learning. You are free to use other similar resources identified during your research.

RULES FOR GOOD GRAPHS

Knowing what type of graph to use with what type of information is crucial. Depending on the nature of the data, some graphs are more appropriate than others. For example, categorical data such as favourite school subjects is best displayed in a bar chart or circle graph, whereas continuous numerical data, such as height, is best illustrated by a line graph or histogram.

The following is a list of general rules to keep in mind when preparing graphs.

A good graph will:

- accurately show the facts
- grab the reader's attention
- complement, or demonstrate, the arguments presented in the text
- have a title, labelled axis, a key and annotations, if appropriate
- be simple and uncluttered
- show data without altering the message within the data
- clearly show any trends, or differences, in the data
- be visually accurate (e.g. if one chart value is 15 and another value is 30, then 30 should be twice the size of 15).

When is it not appropriate to use a graph?

A graph is not always the most appropriate tool with which to present information. Sometimes text or a data table can provide a better explanation for the reader, saving considerable time and effort.

Don't use graphs when:

- the data are very dispersed
- there is insufficient data (only one, two or three data points)
- the data are too numerous
- the data show little or no variation

THINGS TO DO AND THINK ABOUT

As you work through the graphical techniques on pp. 56–63, think about the links that exist within these graphical techniques and between the various other geographical techniques in this study guide:

- data-gathering techniques for physical geography (pp. 8–23)
- data-gathering techniques for human geography (pp. 24–37)
- statistical techniques (pp. 38–53)
- mapping techniques (pp. 64–81)
- coursework (geographical study and geographical issue) (pp. 82–89)
- the question paper (pp. 90–95).

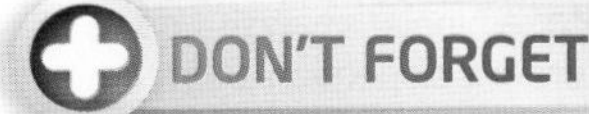

You need to use the most appropriate technique when gathering and processing data.

ONLINE

Head to www.brightredbooks.net to find useful links and information about producing quality graphs and charts and practice exercises.

ONLINE TEST

Test yourself on graphs at www.brightredbooks.net

ONLINE

Check out the section 'What graph should I use?' and the Glossary at www.brightredbooks.net

ONLINE

Check out the examples of mind-maps used to plan research/fieldwork, including the use of graphs at www.brightredbooks.net

ONLINE

Head to www.brightrebbooks.net for further guidelines on using graphs.

BIPOLAR ANALYSIS AND DISPERSION DIAGRAMS

DON'T FORGET 

Refer to the detailed information on pp. 54 and 55 for the equipment needed for a bipolar analysis and to draw a dispersion diagram.

Completing a bipolar analysis record sheet for coastal defences.

VIDEO LINK 

When do you use bipolar analysis? Check out the video at www.brightredbooks.net for a straightforward explanation of bipolar analysis.

DON'T FORGET

Analysis of the results should always refer to relevant and current geographical knowledge and understanding.

ONLINE 

Follow the links at www.brightredbooks.net to sites that provide good information, examples and tests for bipolar analysis.

VIDEO LINK 

See how to draw a dispersion diagram at www.brightredbooks.net

BIPOLAR ANALYSIS

Purpose

Bipolar analysis is a technique used for comparing areas, people or gathered data. It can be used as a visual portrayal of the results of a questionnaire or survey – for example, a comparison between two shopping centres (pp. 30 and 31) or comparing the environment and amenities of three areas (pp. 24 and 25).

Undertaking a bipolar analysis

To undertake a bipolar analysis, you will need to have completed the following steps:

- carried out a questionnaire or survey asking people to compare a range of criteria on a selected scale (e.g. 1–5 or 1–10)
- collated the results of the survey
- calculated the average value for each of the criteria – the values should be rounded up or down to the nearest whole number.

Next:

- construct a table/diagram like the one shown here (or in the video) to plot the averages for your chosen criteria
- plot a dot for each average value under the relevant number in the scale
- join the dots with a line.

Poor-quality shopping environment	1	2	3	4	5	High-quality shopping environment
ugly buildings						attractive buildings
difficult to park						easy to park
expensive to park						free to park
lots of litter						no litter
graffiti						no graffiti
high crime rate						safe, secure area
unsafe for pedestrians						safe for pedestrians
Quality of shopping						**Quality of shopping**
poor-value goods						good value
poor choice of goods						excellent choice of goods
poor quality of goods						high quality of goods
Environmental quality						**Environmental quality**
very dirty						very clean
heavy traffic						no traffic
much derelict land						no derelict land
many high-rise buildings						few high-rise buildings

Centre 1 Centre 2

Example of bipolar analysis.

Analysing a bipolar chart

Once completed, the results can be analysed to highlight their similarities and/or differences. Be aware that the results are based on people's perceptions and beliefs. As such, although useful, they may not be true. Bear this in mind when considering any conclusions from the analysis of the data.

Considerations/limitations of bipolar analysis

Advantages:

- a large amount of data can be plotted in a relatively small space
- patterns can be identified quickly and easily.

Disadvantages:

- the results are based on people's perceptions, which may be biased
- the technique can only be used for two or three areas, otherwise the graph will become cluttered and confusing to analyse.

DISPERSION DIAGRAMS

Purpose

Dispersion diagrams are used to display the main patterns in the distribution of data. The graph shows each value plotted as an individual point against a vertical scale. It shows the range of data and the distribution of each piece of data within that range. It therefore enables a comparison of the degree of clustering of two sets of data – for example, comparing the quality of life of people living in urban areas with that of people living in rural areas.

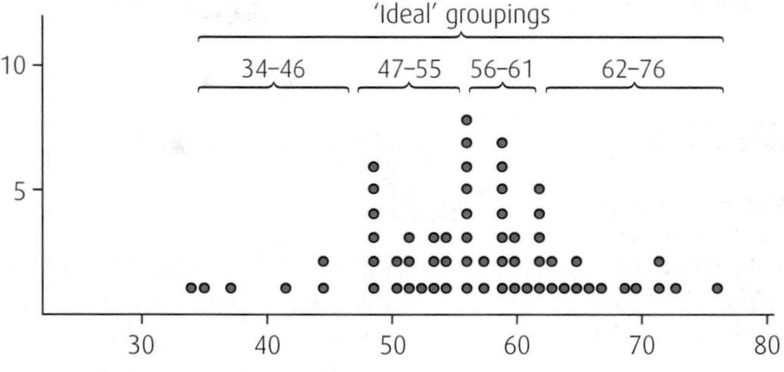

Dispersion diagrams show a range of values in a data set.

Constructing a dispersion diagram

The important features of a dispersion diagram are:

- data sets are placed in one column along the *x*-axis
- a vertical scale is used for the variable on the *y*-axis
- it compares data sets to see whether there is a statistically significant difference between the sets.

Analysing a dispersion diagram

Analysis of a completed dispersion diagram should show the similarities and differences between the data sets. The use of appropriate statistical techniques will allow testing to see whether the differences are statistically significant.

Reference to relevant geographical knowledge and understanding is often required in the interpretation of the data.

Considerations/limitations of dispersion diagrams

Advantages

- show the spread from the mean
- are easily understood
- give an indication of the reliability of the data
- allow the calculation of the mean, range, mode, median, lower quartile, upper quartile and interquartile range
- can compare graphs easily
- anomalies can be shown
- can calculate the standard deviation.

Disadvantages

- data must be in a form that can be placed along a number line
- work better with lots of data
- the standard deviation can easily be manipulated and can be biased.

VIDEO LINK

See how to analyse the results of a dispersion diagram at www.brightredbooks.net

DON'T FORGET

Dispersion diagrams are useful for making comparisons between areas or of one area over a period of time.

ONLINE TEST

Head to www.brightredbooks.net to test yourself on bipolar analysis and dispersion diagrams.

THINGS TO DO AND THINK ABOUT

Refer to the generic advice for graphs on pp. 54 and 55 and the following specific points.

Think about the possible links that bipolar analysis and dispersion diagrams have with other geographical techniques in this study guide.

Bipolar analysis:

- consider what other graphical technique(s) might be used to visualise the data, such as histograms or divided bar graphs
- consider how you might use statistical techniques to enhance the results of the bipolar analysis – for example, the Spearman rank correlation coefficient or the Pearson product moment correlation coefficient.

Dispersion diagrams:

- note the links between this graphical technique and the range of statistical techniques explained on pp. 38–41, such as the median, range, interquartile range and statistical significance
- use Microsoft Excel to create a dispersion graph using a geographical example by following the link at www.brightredbooks.net
- box/whisker plots can be added to further analyse the data and to increase your geographical understanding.

ONLINE

Use the video Point Dispersion Part 2 at www.brightredbooks.net to complete the revision exercise.

KITE DIAGRAMS AND LOGARITHMIC GRAPHS

DON'T FORGET 

Refer to the detailed information on pp. 54 and 55 for the equipment needed to draw kite diagrams and logarithmic graphs.

Sampling using a quadrat.

ONLINE 

The website link at www.brightredbooks.net gives useful information on sampling techniques.

VIDEO LINK 

See how to draw a kite diagram by watching the clip at www.brightredbooks.net

DON'T FORGET 

A kite diagram works by showing how species concentrations change across a study area.

ONLINE 

Follow the links at www.brightredbooks.net to sites that provide good information, examples and tests for kite diagrams.

KITE DIAGRAMS

Purpose

A kite graph displays the density and distribution of plant or animal species in a particular habitat. A kite diagram can be used to show the abundance of key marine species as you move from the shoreline to below the low-tide mark on a rocky shore or can show changes in vegetation coverage near ecosystem boundaries, such as between a meadow and a forest – see pp. 10 and 11 (beach profile), pp. 16 and 17 (slope analysis), pp. 22 and 23 (vegetation analysis) and pp. 80 and 81 (transects).

A quadrat is usually a square made of wire. It may contain further wires to mark off smaller areas inside, such as 5 × 5 or 10 × 10 squares. The organisms within each square, usually plants, can be identified and counted.

Constructing a kite diagram

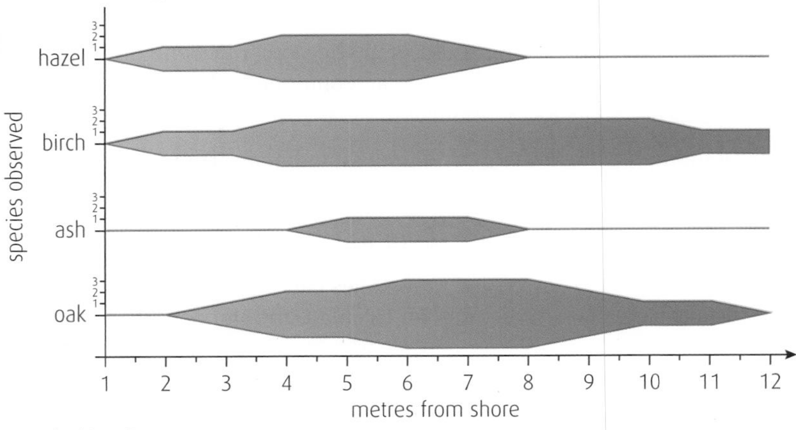

Sample kite diagram.

The data needed to construct a kite diagram are the distance of each quadrat along the transect line and the density of each species of interest in each quadrat.

The important features of a kite diagram are:

- the *x* or horizontal axis shows distance – the length of the transect and the sample points (e.g. every 2 m)
- the *y* or vertical axis shows the observed species
- a kite shape is plotted for each observed species

Analysing a kite diagram

The analysis of a kite diagram should indicate where the various species occur and the frequency of each species. It should also include an explanation of the spatial patterns in the diagram, highlighting changes over the distance of the transect and the possible relationships between individual species and/or other related variables.

Considerations/limitations of kite diagrams

Advantages:

- useful for displaying changes over distance
- visually clear and easy to distinguish one category from another
- comparisons can easily be made.

Disadvantages:

- visually subjective, as the scale influences the visual effect
- only works with a specific range of data
- time-consuming to construct by hand.

Kite diagrams may need to be broken down into sections for larger studies over 100 m. An alternative graphical technique is a histogram.

LOGARITHMIC GRAPHS

Purpose

Logarithmic graphs are used when the values on the scales are so large that they are difficult to show on linear graph paper or when the graph is to be used to compare the rates of growth (exponential growth) of the variables over time. A logarithmic scale increases by multiplications in value rather than additions (e.g. 1, 10, 100, 1000 rather than 1, 2, 3, 4). The value by which the scale is multiplied is usually ten (i.e. log-base 10). Both scales may be logarithmic, or just one scale logarithmic and the other linear (semi-logarithmic graphs).

Semi-logarithmic graphs are commonly used in geography to compare the rates of increase or decrease in economic data, changes in population size, agricultural yields and energy production.

Constructing a logarithmic graph

The important features of a semi-logarithmic graph are:

- the *x*-axis is spaced evenly, as in a linear graph
- the *y*-axis is not spaced evenly – that is, the interval between 20 and 30 is smaller than that between 10 and 20
- the *y*-axis scale increases in cycles of values, with each cycle increasing by a larger amount – for example, each successive cycle has values ten times greater than those in the cycle below.

Analysing a logarithmic graph

When analysing logarithmic graphs, be mindful of the following points:

- whether you are interpreting a two-scale logarithmic or semi- (one-scale) logarithmic graph
- the scale values on the *x*-axis and *y*-axis
- the direction of the line – it is easy to interpret these graphs in the same way as linear graphs and to obtain a completely wrong meaning from the displayed data
- evaluate whether the changes in the line direction actually show an increase, decrease, or a constant value
- a constant proportional rate of change (an exponential change) is represented by a straight line on a logarithmic graph (rather than a curved line on a linear graph) – this means that logarithmic graphs are good for comparing rates of change.

Considerations/limitations of logarithmic graphs

Advantages

- useful for studying data that change exponentially
- can display a much larger range of data than a linear scale
- allow you to see increased detail at smaller values, whereas larger values are compressed
- small values occupy a larger proportion of the scale than larger values
- on a linear scale, unless the graph paper is very large, smaller values would be too small to see properly
- allow comparison between trends in small and large values.

Disadvantages

- zero cannot be plotted
- positive and negative values cannot be plotted on the same graph
- can be difficult to plot values accurately
- difficult to interpret as scale is distorted.

THINGS TO DO AND THINK ABOUT

Refer to the generic advice for graphs on pp. 54 and 55 and the following specific points.

Think about the possible links that kite diagrams and logarithmic graphs have with other geographical techniques in this study guide.

Kite diagram:

- use the Microsoft Excel tutorial to create a kite chart
- use the specially designed kite diagram in Microsoft Excel.

Logarithmic graph:

- use a Microsoft Excel spreadsheet to produce a logarithmic graph
- download and use the Merlin add-on for Microsoft Excel – this is a simple statistics software package.

VIDEO LINK

Watch the video at www.brightredbooks.net to understand the use of logarithmic and semi-logarithmic graphs in geography.

VIDEO LINK

See how to draw a semi-logarithmic graph at www.brightredbooks.net

ONLINE

Download a logarithmic graph template by following the link at www.brightredbooks.net

VIDEO LINK

Watch the video at www.brightredbooks.net to remind yourself of the structure and potential issues when interpreting a logarithmic graph.

DON'T FORGET

Logarithmic graphs allow the comparison of variables that differ enormously in size.

ONLINE TEST

Head to www.brightredbooks.net to revise and test yourself on kite diagrams and logarithmic graphs.

ONLINE

Head to www.brightredbooks.net to find relevant links for the 'Things to do and think about' section.

POLAR GRAPHS AND SYSTEM DIAGRAMS

DON'T FORGET

Refer to the detailed information on pp. 54 and 55 for the equipment needed to draw polar graphs and system diagrams.

POLAR GRAPHS

Purpose

Polar graphs are used to show direction as well as magnitude. They can only be used when the data shows some form of orientation. They have several practical uses in geography for showing a relationship or correlation between two observed variables, such as:

- corries – orientation of corries against altitude or size
- vegetation – aspect of a slope against frequency of vegetation type
- slopes – aspect of the slope against soil variable (pH, water content or humus content)
- retail – location of coffee shops from a central point.

See Advanced Higher SQA past paper 2015 Question 4(c) and refer to pp. 16 and 17 (slope analysis) and pp. 22 and 23 (vegetation analysis).

Polar graphs should not be confused with:

- circular graphs, which can be used to show a variable that is continuous over time (e.g. temperature data – see link at www.brightredbooks.net)
- rose diagrams, which use compass directions or bearings to show observed data (e.g. wind direction – see link at www.brightredbooks.net).

Corrie orientation against altitude in North Wales

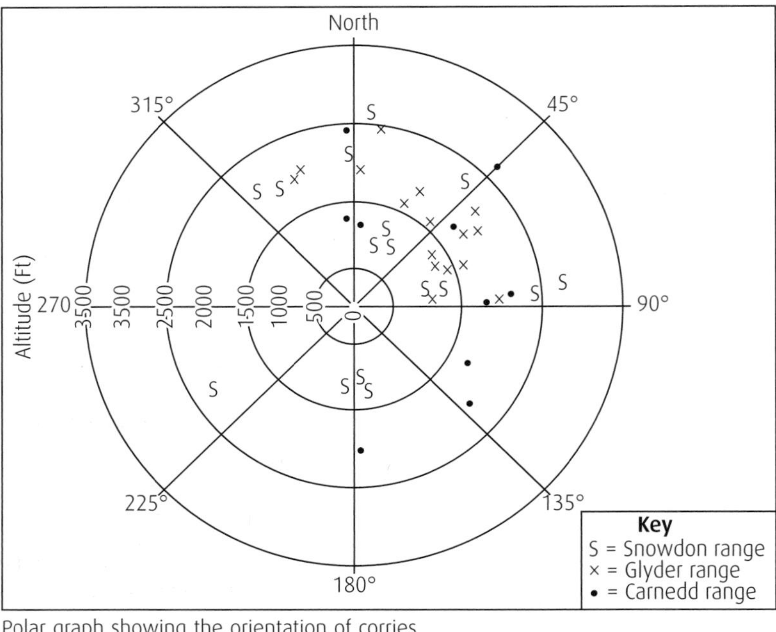

Polar graph showing the orientation of corries.

ONLINE

Find the link to polar graph paper at www.brightredbooks.net

Constructing a polar graph

The important features of a polar graph are:

- a fixed point from where the orientation can be observed – for example, a grid reference on a mountain top – this will become the centre of the graph
- two variables – one is always orientation/direction (e.g. a compass bearing from north) and the second variable is the distance from the fixed point (the centre of the graph) representing any variable quantity (e.g. size or altitude)
- a more comparative dimension could be added to the graph by using different symbols to compare data from several locations superimposed onto one graph.

DON'T FORGET

A specialised graph type is used where one variable is directional.

Follow these steps to complete a polar graph:

- download and print a blank piece of polar graph paper
- add compass directions and/or bearings to the graph – north at the top
- decide on an appropriate scale that covers the range of data (e.g. the radius of the graph)
- plot the scale along the radius
- carefully plot the observed data using a protractor and ruler
- add appropriate labels (e.g. a title and key).

ONLINE

Follow the links at www.brightredbooks.net to sites that provide good information, examples and tests for polar graphs.

Analysing a polar graph

Polar graphs show data in an unfamiliar way, so care should be taken when interpreting these graphs to take into account the nature of their construction. You should be able to describe the patterns in the data presented in the graph, highlighting, in particular, the special dimensions/orientations of the results.

contd

Considerations/limitations of polar graphs

Advantages

- useful when one variable is directional
- variables within the diagram can be compared
- visual – patterns can be identified quickly and easily
- can compare multiple sets of data
- lots of data can be put on one graph and compared.

Disadvantages

- only useful with a limited type of data
- hard to make a suitable scale
- polar graphs can distort the higher values, making them difficult to interpret
- no statistical test can be linked to them
- hard to spot anomalies.

ONLINE

Head to www.brightredbooks.net for links and videos for constructing system diagrams.

SYSTEM DIAGRAMS

Purpose

System diagrams (flowcharts) are simple graphical devices used to communicate complex relationships. In some instances, the system diagram may be overlaid onto a physical representation of a landscape.

System diagrams are often used as planning tools to organise a programme of work or as a way of summarising key information.

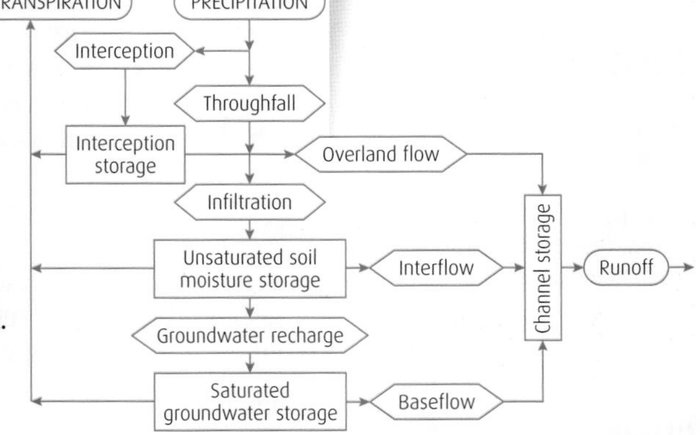

Example of a system diagram.

Constructing a system diagram

The important features of a system diagram are:

- the key constituent parts/stages within the system are usually boxed off and arranged in the order of movement through the system
- lines link the constituent parts of the system
- arrows on the lines show the direction of movement through the system.

Analysing a system diagram

The analysis of system diagrams that are well drawn and clear is straightforward. Begin at the start and follow through, using the links and arrows to identify each stage in turn. Where options or alternative routes exist, the reasons for, and the impact of, these routes should be explained. Return routes back through the process should also be identified and the impact or effect explained.

Considerations/limitations of system diagrams

Advantages

- an important tool for planning and laying out a process
- provide an overview of the system
- demonstrate the relationship between various stages
- convenient method of communication, as they are easy to read and follow
- key features are easily identified
- they provide logical paths/options.

Disadvantages

- require a lot of planning to ensure all stages are included
- can become complex if too much information is displayed
- take a long time to produce.

DON'T FORGET

System diagrams can communicate complex relationships simply.

DON'T FORGET

Remember that the stages within the system diagram are part of the whole, and consequently the analysis should refer not only to the constituent parts but also to the whole diagram as one entity.

ONLINE TEST

Head to www.brightredbooks.net to revise and test yourself on polar graphs and system diagrams.

VIDEO LINK

Check out the clip Advanced Higher Geography Skills - System Diagrams and Bipolar Analysis at www.brightredbooks.net

THINGS TO DO AND THINK ABOUT

Refer to the generic advice for graphs on pp. 54 and 55 and the following specific points. Think about the possible links that polar graphs and system diagrams have with other geographical techniques in this study guide. Visit the Digital Zone to: use the links and videos at www.brightredbooks.net to learn how to produce other radial diagrams; use a Microsoft Excel spreadsheet to create a system diagram by following the links at www.brightredbooks.net.

SCATTER GRAPHS AND TRIANGULAR GRAPHS

DON'T FORGET 

Refer to the detailed information on pp. 54 and 55 for the equipment needed to draw scatter graphs and triangular graphs.

VIDEO LINK 

When do you use a scatter graph? Check out the video at www.brightredbooks.net for a straightforward explanation of the purpose of scatter graphs.

VIDEO LINK 

See how to draw a scatter graph by watching the clip at www.brightredbooks.net

DON'T FORGET 

Add the best-fit line to indicate a possible relationship between two variables.

ONLINE 

Follow the links at www.brightredbooks.net to sites providing good information, examples and tests for scatter graphs.

SCATTER GRAPHS

Purpose

Scatter graphs are used to show a relationship or correlation between two sets of paired data (variables) – for example, population size and number of services, or distance from the source of a river and average pebble size (e.g. pp. 14 and 15, pebble analysis).

Constructing a scatter graph

The important features of a scatter graph are:

- the x or horizontal axis is the independent variable – the variable affecting the change
- the y or vertical axis is the dependent variable – the variable affected by the change
- the line of best fit is a straight line drawn to represent the direction and nature of the correlation.

Analysing a scatter graph

You should be able to describe the patterns in data presented in graphs and tables of results. Reference to relevant geographical knowledge and understanding is often required in the interpretation of the data.

When analysing scatter graphs, consider the following points:

- a positive correlation occurs when an increase in one variable is matched by an increase in the other variable
- a negative correlation occurs when an increase in one variable is matched by a decrease in the other variable
- the line of best fit indicates the general trend and is drawn in such a way as to keep the distances from the line to the points equal above and below the line – the type of correlation revealed by the best-fit line is known as a geographical correlation
- points well away from the line of best fit are known as residuals or anomalies and should be ignored, although they should be referred to in written analyses of the graph.

Scatterplots and correlation

Correlation – indicates a relationship (connection) between two sets of data

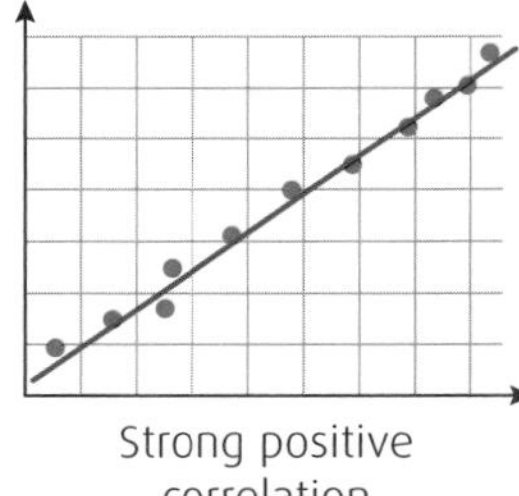

Strong positive correlation

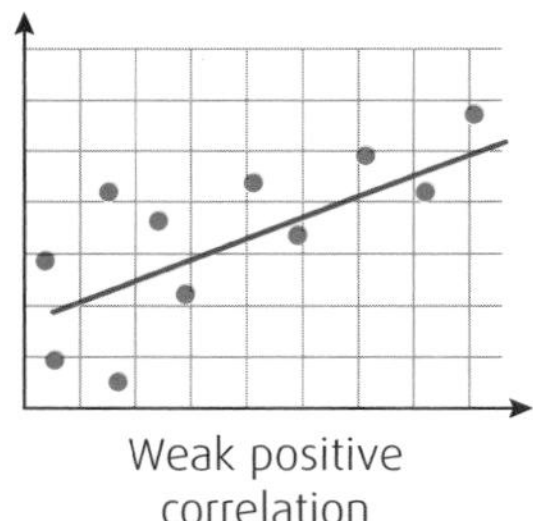

Weak positive correlation

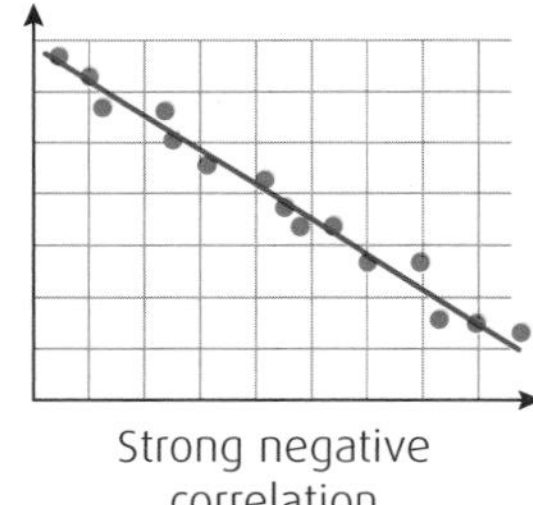

Strong negative correlation

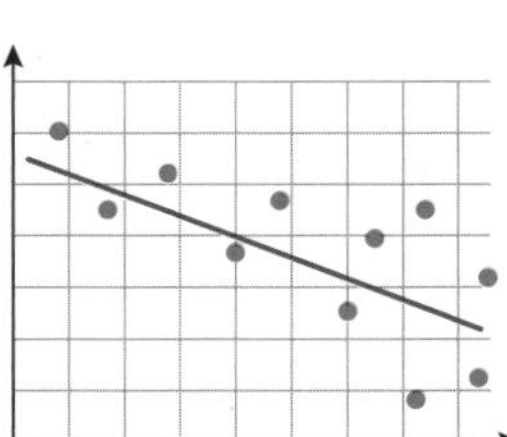

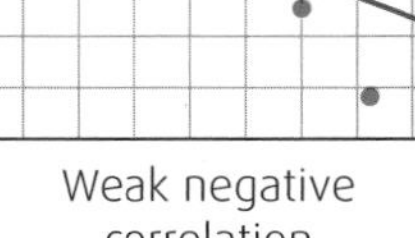

Weak negative correlation

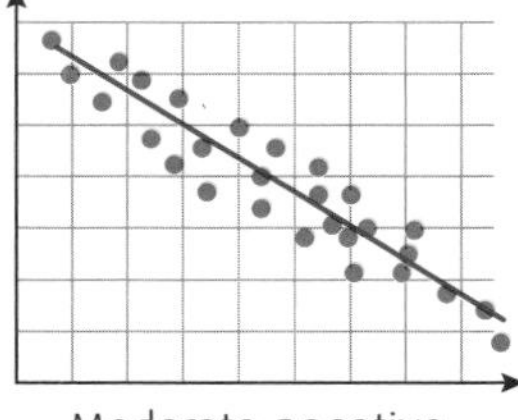

Moderate negative correlation

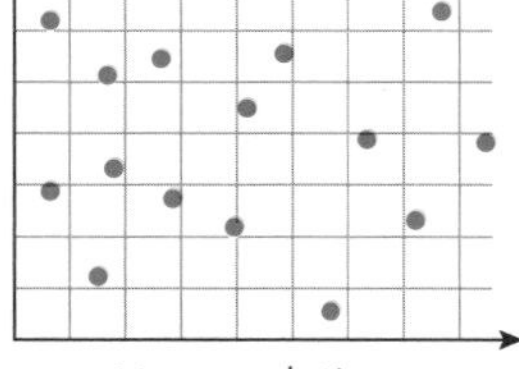

No correlation

Examples of correlation using scatter graphs.

Considerations/limitations of scatter graphs

Advantages:

- large amounts of data can be plotted in a relatively small space
- patterns can be identified quickly and easily
- anomalies can be identified.

Disadvantages:

- can only be used to display two variables
- you can easily make mistakes when plotting large numbers of points
- the best-fit line may indicate a misleading relationship.

TRIANGULAR GRAPHS

Purpose

Triangular graphs are used to represent different types of data and are useful when three components are involved. The most important properties of the graphs are that each axis represents a percentage value, and the angles are drawn at about 60° to make data more readable. Triangular graphs can also indicate the relative dominance of one component over the others and can be easily updated when changes occur in the data. They are useful when identifying changes over time.

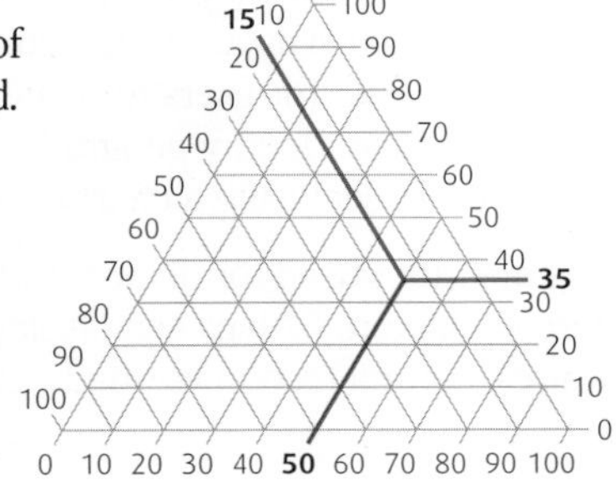

Constructing a triangular graph

The important features of a triangular graph are:

- each axis is divided into 100, representing percentages
- lines are drawn at angles of 60° from each 100–0% axis to carry the values
- the data used must be in the form of three components, each component representing a percentage value, and the three component percentage values must add up to 100%.

Analysing a triangular graph

Use three different colours to accentuate the lines representing each of the components to make reading the graph easier. The most important aspect to remember is that the lines corresponding to each component are formed at 60° and should not be confused with the lines of the other components.

Considerations/limitations of triangular graphs

Advantages

- very useful if three components are to be compared
- a large amount of data can be plotted
- dominant characters can be identified
- clusters emerge after plotting, enabling the classification/identification of trends.

Disadvantages

- data must be presented as percentages
- difficult to interpret
- limited range of data.

VIDEO LINK

See how to draw a triangular graph at www.brightredbooks.net

ONLINE

Download a triangular graph template by following the link at www.brightredbooks.net

DON'T FORGET

Triangular graphs only work where there are three variables in percentage form.

ONLINE TEST

Head to www.brightredbooks.net to test yourself on scatter graphs and triangular graphs.

ONLINE

Use the OECD iLibrary to source data sets. The link can be found at www.brightredbooks.net

THINGS TO DO AND THINK ABOUT

Refer to the generic advice for graphs on p. 54 and the following specific points.

Think about the possible links that scatter and triangular graphs have with other geographical techniques in this study guide.

Scatter graphs:

- use linear regression analysis to calculate the regression line to achieve a greater level of accuracy (pp. 50 and 51)
- assuming there are sufficient data, you could use the Spearman rank correlation coefficient or the Pearson product moment correlation coefficient to test whether there is a significant statistical relationship (pp. 46–49).

Triangular graphs:

- use the tri-plot in a Microsoft Excel spreadsheet for the preparation of triangular (ternary) diagrams for particle shape and trivariate data by following the link at www.brightredbooks.net
- expand your knowledge of triangular graphs by further reading at www.brightredbooks.net

MAPS AND MAP-BASED DIAGRAMS

GENERAL ADVICE ON THE USE OF MAPS AND MAP-BASED DIAGRAMS

PURPOSE

The mapping techniques explained on pp. 64–81 are those you are expected to know and understand for the examination. Within the context of the unit on geographical skills and the coursework (the geographical study and geographical issue), you are free to use any appropriate and relevant mapping technique. Maps are an excellent means of presenting information. Not only are they visually attractive, they also:

- make it easier for users to relate data to a location
- help users to identify geographical trends and patterns in the data that would be difficult to see using a chart or a table.

Maps are often used for demonstration (i.e. display) purposes rather than as a source of reference material. Maps can display political boundaries, population numbers, physical features, natural resources, roads, climate, elevation (topography) and economic activity.

DON'T FORGET 

Don't allow your learning to get lost in a bundle of internet links.

DON'T FORGET 

Knowing how to convey information on a map is important in presenting data.

EQUIPMENT

The equipment needed to produce a map or map-based diagram includes:

- paper, pencil and an eraser
- a computer with Microsoft Excel or a similar software package
- a research/fieldwork notebook
- data recorded during research
- source maps
- data collected during fieldwork.

ONLINE 

Use the link at www.brightredbooks.net to revise your basic map skills.

PRESENTATION

As part of your learning, it is important that you complete the mapping techniques on paper by hand, showing the full detailed application of the particular technique (see worked examples for each of the mapping techniques on pp. 66–81). The other methods illustrated are optional for use within your coursework.

Be methodical to ensure that no mistake is made in entering data.

You are expected to explain in detail the patterns and relationships displayed by the mapping technique(s) used within the context of the problem. This analysis of the map(s) is expected to refer to relevant and current geographical knowledge and understanding.

Within the context of the coursework (geographical study and geographical issue), you are free to use any relevant mapping technique.

Candidates who use an appropriate and relevant mapping technique within the context of their coursework are more likely to achieve higher marks. It is not about the number of mapping techniques you include, but their relevance and sophistication. You are expected to use more complex mapping techniques that show relationships or differences and allow more detailed analyses.

The links to video and online materials are for illustrative purposes and can help to support your learning. You are free to use other similar resources that you might identify during your research.

Rules for good maps

Knowing what type of map to use with what type of information is crucial. Depending on the nature of the data, some maps are more appropriate than others.

DON'T FORGET 

You need to use the most appropriate mapping technique for your data.

ONLINE 

Check out the rules for a good map at www.brightredbooks.net

ONLINE 

Head to the Digital Zone for useful links and videos on maps and annotations.

ONLINE 

Check out the examples of mind-maps used to plan research/fieldwork, including the use of maps at www.brightredbooks.net

ANNOTATIONS

Purpose

Annotation means 'adding notes' to photographs, overlays, field sketches, graphs, maps diagrams or data tables to emphasise or add to the information shown.

Methodology

This can be achieved by:

- writing on the photograph, map, sketch or diagram – for example, when undertaking fieldwork
- using lines and arrows to link text boxes positioned around a photograph, map, sketch, diagram, graph or table of statistics – for example, during the processing of collected data to establish links between the text and illustration
- creating an overlay (tracing paper or acetate sheet) that covers the photograph, map, sketch, diagram or graph – for example, to identify key features/factors.

We need to be clear about the difference between labelling and annotating.

Labelling is when you identify something – for example, the River Forth.

Annotating is when you further explain your point, highlighting/explaining something within the illustration – for example, 'the River Forth has flooded adjacent farmland because the embankment collapsed following prolonged heavy rain and higher than expected tides'.

Geography textbooks are full of all kinds of illustrations that have been annotated. Have a look at the illustrations in a few textbooks and see which ones are labelled or annotated.

Considerations/limitations of annotations

Advantages:

- thoughtful annotations bring out key features or points, showing readers that you understand the context
- annotations can be linked to the context in the written paragraph, enhancing the argument in the text
- annotations allow you to enhance an existing photograph, map or diagram to highlight aspects linked to your chosen context.

Disadvantages:

- it can be hard to find enough to write
- it requires more space than just captioning a photo
- it takes time and thought to plan the arrangement of annotations
- you need to strike a balance to ensure the annotations are more than just labels without writing too much and providing excessive detail
- too much information can make the map, sketch, photograph or diagram look overcrowded or detract from the image.

THINGS TO DO AND THINK ABOUT

Refer to the generic advice for maps and map-based diagrams on pp. 64 and 65 and the following specific points.

As you work through the mapping techniques on pp. 66–81, think about the links that exist within the mapping techniques and between the various other geographical techniques explained within this study guide:

- data-gathering techniques for physical geography (pp. 8–23)
- data-gathering techniques for human geography (pp. 24–37)
- statistical techniques (pp. 38–53)
- graphical techniques (pp. 54–63)
- coursework (geographical study and geographical issue) (pp. 82–89)
- question paper (pp. 90–95).

ONLINE

Follow the links at www.brightredbooks.net to sites providing good information, examples and tests for annotating.

ONLINE

Check out the section 'What map should I use?' at www.brightredbooks.net

VIDEO LINK

Check out the video on how to annotate a photo at www.brightredbooks.net

DON'T FORGET

Warning: too many overlays can become complicated and confuse the message.

VIDEO LINK

Check out the video on how to draw a field sketch at www.brightredbooks.net

ONLINE

For examples of annotations, head to www.brightredbooks.net

ONLINE

Check out the Glossary for this study guide at www.brightredbooks.net

CHOROPLETH MAPS

DON'T FORGET 

Refer to the detailed information on pp. 64 and 65 for the equipment needed to draw a choropleth map.

ONLINE 

Use the link on the Digital Zone to find out more about choropleth maps.

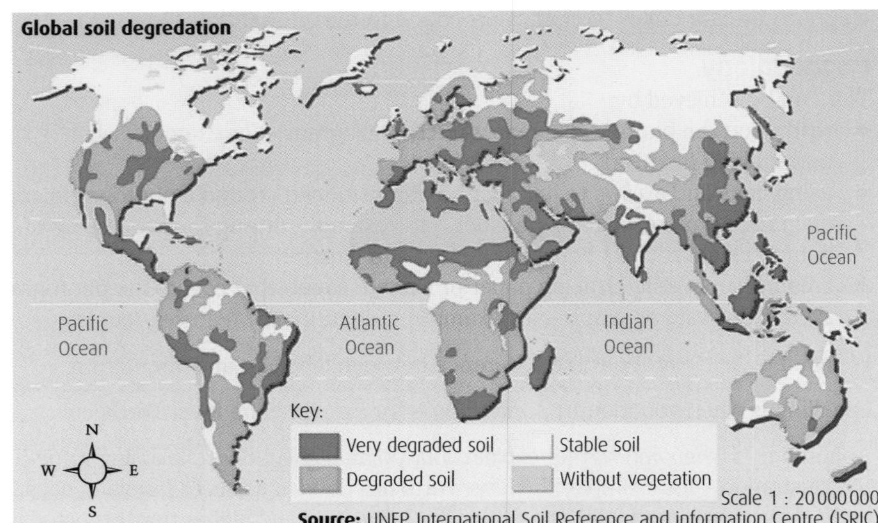

Example of a choropleth map.

PURPOSE

Choropleth maps are one of the most widely used techniques in displaying geographical data. Choropleth maps use a system of colour, greyscale, or line-density shading, to illustrate how the density of the data changes from area to area. They are maps on which areas are shaded according to a pre-arranged key. Each shading, or colour type, represents a range of values or bands, allowing the user to identify similarities and differences. They are especially appropriate for showing standardised data such as rates, densities or percentages.

Choropleth maps can be used to represent:

- density information expressed per unit area – for example, population per square kilometre
- differences in area data – for example, land ownership
- differences in land use – for example, the amount of recreational land or type of forest cover
- the percentage of eligible voters – for example, voters per ward or constituency
- tax rates expressed as percentages.

ONLINE 

Use the link at www.brightredbooks.net to help you understand the types of choropleth maps that exist and which type to choose for your data.

VIDEO LINK 

Watch the video 'How to make a choropleth map' at www.brightredbooks.net to see how to construct this type of map.

CONSTRUCTING A CHOROPLETH MAP

Use the following guide and the video on the Digital Zone to help you to construct a choropleth map:

1. Draw or source a base map with defined areas linked to a data set – for example, a map of New Zealand showing farming areas or regions.
2. Calculate standardised values for the areas on the base map (e.g. the farming areas).
3. Record these values in a table for reference – for example, a table showing farming regions and the number of cows.
4. Review the spread of values and decide the appropriate number of bands to best illustrate the data.
   A balance needs to be made between:
   - too few bands, which could over-generalise the data and provide little visual information to analyse
   - too many bands, which could make the map overcomplicated and therefore making it difficult to recognise and meaningfully analyse differences in colour or shading.
5. The following will assist you in deciding how to band the data depending on the type of information being mapped:
   - fixed intervals where a data set has meaningful thresholds – for example, 0–9, 10–11
   - fixed intervals based on mathematical relationships (e.g. percentiles) – you could use quintiles, whereby the bottom 20% of values fall into one class and the next 20% into another, and so on

contd

- polarised ranges, whereby categories cluster towards one (or both) ends of the range of values – for example, to highlight deprivation, you might decide that the most prosperous 80% of areas are one shade, but the most deprived areas are highlighted by having different shades for the poorest 20, 10 and 5% of areas
- intervals designed to reflect the natural breaks in the data sets – for example, if data values tend to cluster into distinct groups, you may wish to adjust the ranges so that all those areas falling into a particular group are shaded in the same colour.

At the simplest level, arithmetic classes are obtained by dividing the range of values by the number of classes. This method has problems if the data is skewed; it is important that no single class occupies too large an area.

6. Choose a logical system of shading or colouring – for example:
   - for monochrome maps, use graded tones from light (low) to dark (high)
   - for coloured maps, use a gradation of colour along a range, rather than having completely unrelated colours for each category
   - note that it is not easy for readers to distinguish more than four shades of one colour
   - use light colours for low values and darker colours for high values
   - be aware that certain colours may have natural associations (e.g. red with debt)
   - white is generally used to indicate areas where data is missing or unavailable – it is therefore inadvisable to use white to represent any part of your range of actual values.
7. Add a key, title, scale, compass direction and the data source to the map.

Shaded maps can emphasise large areas much more than small ones – for example, highlighting rural areas over urban areas.

ONLINE

Follow the links at www.brightredbooks.net to sites that provide good information, examples and tests for choropleth maps.

ONLINE TEST

Head to www.brightredbooks.net to test yourself on choropleth maps.

ONLINE

Follow the link on the Digital Zone for the Geographical Base Map Library.

ANALYSING A CHOROPLETH MAP

When analysing choropleth maps, you should be able to explain, within the context of the question/data, the spatial patterns illustrated in the mapped data with reference to relevant background geographical knowledge and understanding. Any anomalous results should be explained by referring to other sources or research.

To fully appreciate the displayed data, always consider the nature of the map's construction and use an atlas to obtain a wider perspective, taking into account that:

- the values in each area are average values and do not take into account other factors (e.g. relief, climate and economic activity)
- boundaries between areas are artificial divisions between the colours, whereas, in reality, the change will be more gradual
- the completed map hides any variation within an area.

CONSIDERATIONS/LIMITATIONS OF CHOROPLETH MAPS

Advantages

- are visually effective – can show a large amount of information and general patterns
- have levels of shading/colour that represent a range of values
- have groupings that can be flexible to accommodate the spread of values
- have categories that provide a clear visual comparison of patterns
- illustrate cause-and-effect interpretations from the map data
- choropleth maps use averages, so can be used to compare areas, regions or countries.

Disadvantages

- the interval/class size needs to be chosen carefully
- it can be difficult to distinguish between different shades
- there could be variations
- choropleth maps are often not suitable for showing total values – proportional symbol overlays (pp. 70 and 71) are one solution to this problem.

THINGS TO DO AND THINK ABOUT

Refer to the generic advice for graphs on pp. 64 and 65 and the following specific points.

Think about the possible links that choropleth maps have with other geographical techniques in this study guide.

Check out the links on the Digital Zone about using geographical information systems.

DOT MAPS

DON'T FORGET 

Refer to the detailed information on pp. 64 and 65 for the equipment needed to draw a dot map.

PURPOSE

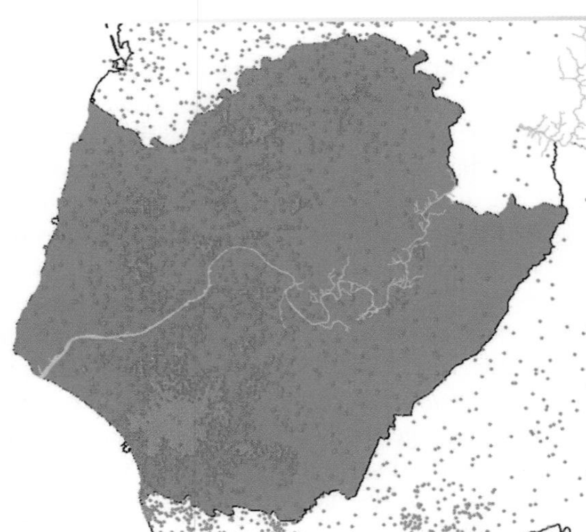

Example of a dot map.

Dot maps are useful for showing the density and indicating the distribution of a variable, such as population. Dot maps are used to show a phenomenon when both the value and location are known – for example, the distribution of dairy farms. Dot maps create a visual impression of density by placing a dot, or some other symbol, in the approximate location of the variable being mapped. Dot maps should only be used for raw data, not for standardised data or percentages.

The important features of a dot map are:

- the graphical size of each dot
- the value associated with each dot
- the distribution of the dots within the map area

For example, you might stipulate that each dot is two pixels in diameter and that each dot represents 100 people. In general, many small dots, each representing relatively few instances of the attribute, are more effective than a few large dots, but such maps are more tedious to construct.

Constructing a dot map

Use the following guide and the video to help construct a dot map.

1. Source a base map showing the geographical area relating to the data.
2. Decide the value of the dot – this should be small enough to have some dots in all areas of the map.
3. Decide on the dot size by considering the dot value and the scale of the map.
4. Place the appropriate number of dots on the map for each area considering that:
   - the dots must be consistent in shape and size
   - the placement of dots must be guided by prior knowledge of the factors that affect the distribution
   - place some dots in boundary zones between statistical areas
   - the dots should be placed at random in high density areas
   - the dots should be allocated to areas of known importance in low density areas
5. Add a key, title, scale and direction to the map.

VIDEO LINK 

Check out the video on how to make a dot map at www.brightredbooks.net

Analysing a dot map

When analysing dot maps, you should be able to explain, within the context of the question/data, the spatial patterns illustrated in the mapped data with reference to relevant background geographical knowledge and understanding. Any anomalous results should be explained by referring to other sources or research.

contd

To fully appreciate the displayed data, always consider the nature of the map's construction and use an atlas to obtain a wider perspective, taking into account that:

- all data points have an equal value
- the scale value used may result in some areas with no dot, which might not be truly accurate
- where the dot represents a scaled value, low density places are under-represented
- it is difficult to obtain exact, accurate values in high density places, particularly when dots merge

Considerations/limitations of dot maps

Advantages:

- if well-constructed, dot maps show distributions and comparative densities
- it is easier to show variations in the distribution of a wide variety of commodities if the dot map is presented using different colours
- dot maps are used to represent a wide range of items, such as populations and the value of minerals and crops
- dot maps are easier to construct than proportional symbols maps (p. 70 and 71)
- it is easy to compare the distribution of items by considering the concentration of dots
- it is easy to interpret data by counting the number of dots multiplied by the dot value to obtain the total value of a given area

Disadvantages:

- developing a dot map is time consuming, especially marking the dots on the map
- when the scale is small, many dots are drawn, which may cause overcrowding and difficulties in counting
- in cases where there is an even distribution of dots on a map, there may be a false impression that the distribution is the same over the represented area
- locating dots on a map is a personal and subjective decision and two maps prepared by two different people using the same data are rarely identical
- the construction of dot maps involves tedious calculations, especially when determining the number of dots

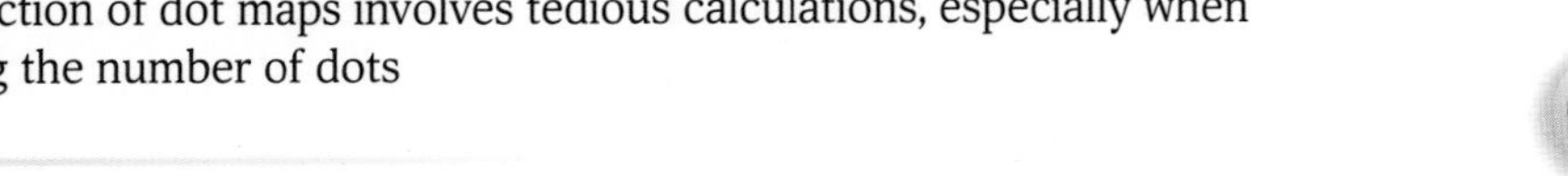

THINGS TO DO AND THINK ABOUT

Refer to the generic advice for graphs on pp. 64 and 65 and the following specific points.

Think about the possible links that dot maps have with other geographical techniques in this study guide.

Use a located proportional-symbols map (pp. 70 and 71) as an alternative to a dot map.

ONLINE

Follow the link on the Digital Zone for the Geographical Base Map Library.

DON'T FORGET

The limitations of dot maps include the difficulty of counting large numbers of dots to obtain a precise value and the need to have a large amount of initial information before drawing the map.

DON'T FORGET

You can use other symbols instead of dots, such as squares, triangles or even letters.

ONLINE TEST

Head to www.brightredbooks.net to test yourself on dot maps.

PROPORTIONAL-SYMBOLS MAPS

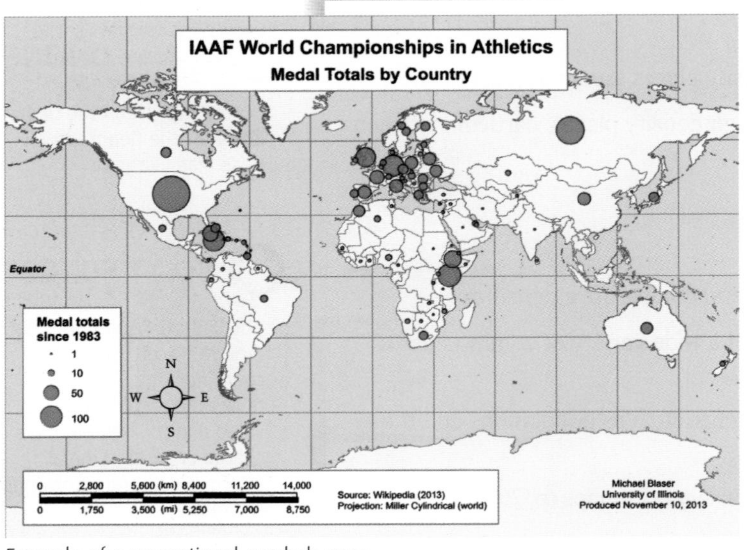

Example of a proportional-symbols map.

PURPOSE

Proportional-symbols maps use scaled symbols according to the data they represent. If you need to represent point data and you want to show not only the distribution, but also spatial variations, then a proportional-symbols map may be suitable. The most common symbols used are bars, circles and squares, although you can use anything as long as the symbols are drawn in proportion to the size of the variable being represented – for example:

- human figures to show military strength
- trains to show the number of trains in an area
- factories to represent industrial output.

As a general rule, make sure that the area, rather than linear proportions such as radius or the length of a side, is the scaled parameter – for example:

- if there are four times as many people in area A than in area B, then the area of the symbol for area A should be four times greater than the area of the symbol for area B
- if the symbol is a circle, then the radius of the area A symbol should be twice the size because area scales with the square of the radius.

DON'T FORGET

Refer to the detailed information on pp. 64 and 65 for the equipment needed to draw a proportional-symbols map.

CONSTRUCTING A PROPORTIONAL-SYMBOLS MAP

DATA COLLECTION POINT	VALUE	SQUARE ROOT OF VALUE
1	200	14·14
2	150	12·25
3	120	10·95
4	57	7·55
5	160	12·65
6	20	4·47

Table A: example of data for a proportional-circles map.

The following example is based on constructing a proportional-circles map, but the procedure is the same for any proportional-symbols map.

1. Organise your data into a table (see Table A).
2. Calculate the square root of each piece of data – these values are used to calculate the radius of each circular symbol.
3. On squared paper, draw out an axis that is large enough to include all your square-root values.

   0 1 2 3 4 5 6 7

4. At the highest end of the scale, draw a circle as large as you can reasonably make it (this can be a bit of a balancing act – a larger circle will give more contrast between values but must be able to fit onto your finished map).
5. Draw a diagonal line from the centre of the circle to the axis where the value is 0.
6. Stick both your scale and the square-root value table to your map (on the back if you cannot fit it on the front).
7. Now use your scale to set your compasses to the correct radius (centre point to the edge) for each square-root value – see the example using a square-root value of 4.
8. Draw the circle on your map so that the data-collection point is located at the centre of your circle. Repeat for each data-collection point.
9. Add a key/legend, title, scale, compass direction and data source to the map.

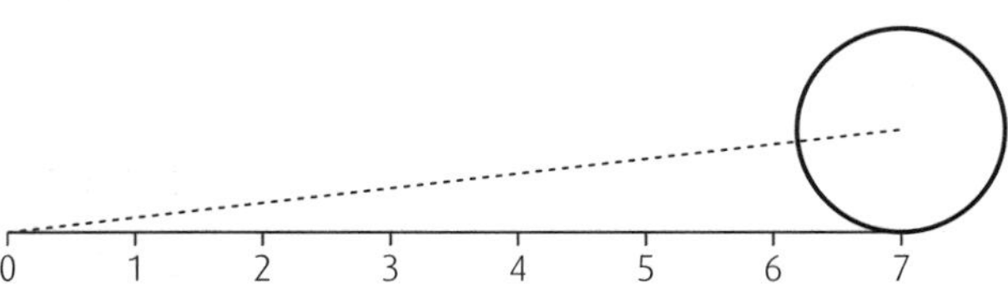

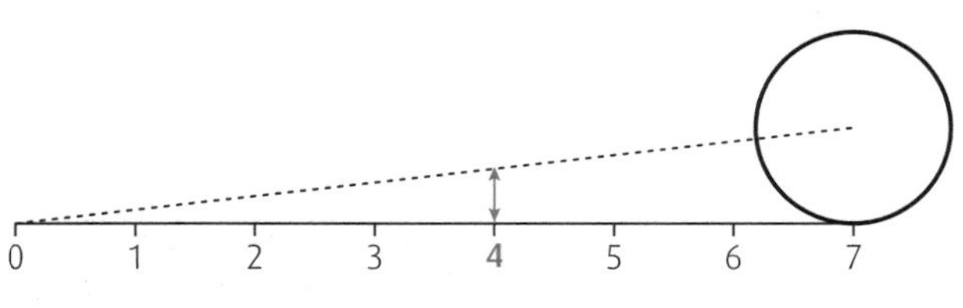

contd

Create three or four extra symbols for round numbers near the bottom, middle and top of your range of values for a legend – for example, if the original values range from 122 500 to 20 250 000 (giving square roots ranging from 350 to 4500), you might use values of 200 000, 5 000 000 and 20 000 000 in your legend.

You could extend the complexity of the proportional-circles map by adding a choropleth scale as follows:

1. Divide your raw data into groups (e.g. three groups) – these do not need to be even, but must incorporate all values from 0 to above your highest value.
2. Draw and label a scale on your map, add three boxes and write the corresponding values next to them.
3. Pick a colour, and shade each box in your scale, using the lightest shade for the lowest values and gradually getting darker to represent the highest values.
4. Shade your proportional circles to correspond to your choropleth scale.

Shade	Value
(light)	=0–5·9
(medium)	6–19
(dark)	20+

Use this link at www.brightredbooks.net to read about the range of different proportional-symbols maps.

See how to draw a proportional-symbols map by watching the clip at www.brightredbooks.net

ANALYSING A PROPORTIONAL-SYMBOLS MAP

When analysing proportional-symbols maps, you should be able to explain, within the context of the question/data, the spatial patterns illustrated in the mapped data with reference to relevant background geographical knowledge and understanding. Any anomalous results should be explained by referring to other sources or research.

To fully appreciate the displayed data, always consider the nature of the map's construction and use an atlas to obtain a wider perspective, taking into account that:

- you need to take particular care when reading the key/legend
- the circles in each area are based on the square root of the original values
- the symbols are proportional in value – for example, a value twice as high needs a symbol with double the surface area
- although the map is good for showing 'big and small' and giving an idea of where events are concentrated, it is less effective for comparison across a range – this is because it is difficult for the human eye to interpret the relative size of two-dimensional objects (although a good key will help).

Follow the link on the Digital Zone for the Geographical Base Map Library.

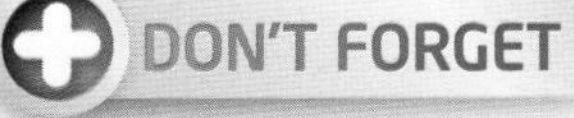

Remember to use the square roots to calculate the symbol sizes for the legend, but label them with the original values!

CONSIDERATIONS/LIMITATIONS OF PROPORTIONAL-SYMBOLS MAPS

Advantages

- useful for illustrating differences between many places
- summarise a large data set in visual form
- easy to read because each symbol is proportional to its value
- data are associated with a specific location
- allow a visual check of the reasonableness or accuracy of calculations.

Disadvantages

- difficult to calculate actual value (if not shown)
- time-consuming to construct
- the size of the symbol may obscure the location or mean less accurate positioning on the maps
- do not reveal key assumptions, causes, effects or patterns
- data could be easily manipulated to yield false impressions.

DON'T FORGET

Proportional-symbols are widely used in business and media to illustrate data.

Test yourself on proportional-symbols maps at www.brightredbooks.net

THINGS TO DO AND THINK ABOUT

Refer to the generic advice for graphs on pp. 64 and 65 and the following specific points.
Think about the possible links that proportional-symbols maps have with other geographical techniques in this study guide, including:

- interview design and implementation (pp. 26 and 27)
- questionnaire design and implementation (pp. 32 and 33)
- nearest-neighbour analysis (pp. 52 and 53)
- bipolar analysis (pp. 56 and 57)
- flow-line maps (desire lines) (pp. 76 and 77).

SPHERE-OF-INFLUENCE MAPS

DON'T FORGET

Refer to the detailed information on pp. 64 and 65 for the equipment needed to draw a sphere-of-influence map.

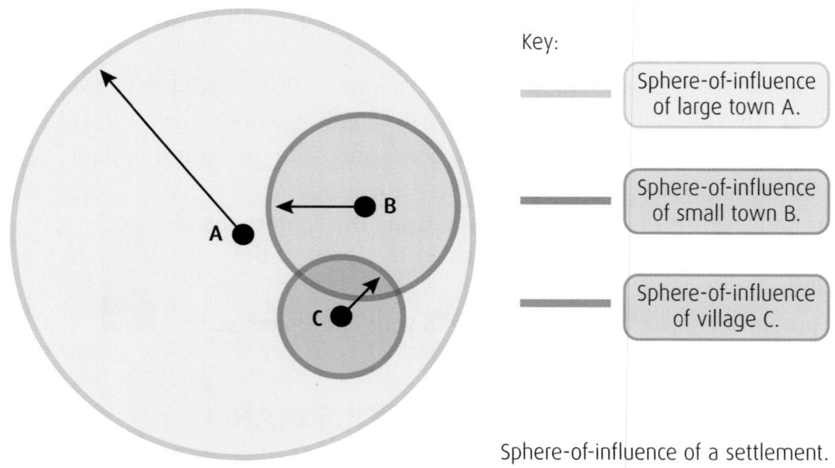

Sphere-of-influence of a settlement.

VIDEO LINK

To find out more about spheres of influence, watch the video on the Digital Zone.

ONLINE

Check out the link for more on this topic at www.brightredbooks.net

VIDEO LINK

See how to draw a sphere-of-influence map by watching the clip at www.brightredbooks.net

PURPOSE

A sphere-of-influence map is used to show the spatial extent, or impact, of a place or geographical event on its surrounding environment. These maps can be drawn using data from either physical or human geography:

- physical geography – for example, a deep depression over the North Sea will have an extensive sphere-of-influence on the weather over much of the UK
- human geography – the number of visitors to a music festival, sporting event, village fete or county agricultural show will have a sphere-of-influence on the surrounding area.

The size and shape of a sphere-of-influence map may depend on related factors, such as the travel time, relief (topography) and transport networks, as well as the specific aspect of the place or event being studied.

The influence exerted tends to decrease with distance – for example, noise from planes taking off and landing creates nuisance close to the airport, which tends to extend in a linear pattern under the flight paths, although at some distance from the airport the nuisance becomes minimal and is unnoticeable beyond a certain distance.

CONSTRUCTING A SPHERE-OF-INFLUENCE MAP

Before attempting to construct a sphere-of-influence map, you need to undertake research to collect and collate information, such as using interviews (interview design and implementation, pp. 26 and 27) or questionnaires (questionnaire design and implementation, pp. 32 and 33) to obtain a data set.

ANALYSING A SPHERE-OF-INFLUENCE MAP

When analysing a sphere-of-influence map, you should be able to explain, within the context of the question/data, the spatial patterns illustrated in the mapped data with reference to relevant background geographical knowledge and understanding. Any anomalous results should be explained by referring to other sources or research.

To fully appreciate the displayed data, always consider the nature of the map's construction and use an atlas to obtain a wider perspective.

A map showing a large sphere-of-influence for a service centre (e.g. a supermarket or town) means that this point is important and will have a wide range of services and functions.

CONSIDERATIONS/LIMITATIONS OF SPHERE-OF-INFLUENCE MAPS

Advantages

Sphere-of-influence maps can show:

- differences between out-of-town shopping centres and those within a central business district
- changing retail provision and shopper behaviour
- the capacity and adequacy of services for a chosen area
- social or economic influences within a defined area
- existing and planned land use in an area, including agricultural land and open spaces
- the need for public services in an area
- the impact of new retail developments – for example, the case for and against the development and its potential positive and negative impacts.

Disadvantages

- the map assumes the whole region/area has the same value, but there could be variations
- no account is taken of the influence of the physical/human landscape in determining the extent of the area influenced – for example, rivers as barriers or roads as assets to communication
- the time required to design and implement suitable methods to collect relevant information, such as interviews and questionnaires.

ONLINE

Follow the link on the Digital Zone for the Geographical Base Map Library.

ONLINE

Follow the links and view the videos at www.brightredbooks.net for sites that provide good information, examples and tests for sphere-of-influence maps.

THINGS TO DO AND THINK ABOUT

Refer to the generic advice for graphs on pp. 64 and 65 and the following specific points.

Think about the possible links that sphere-of-influence maps have with other geographical techniques in this study guide:

- interview design and implementation (pp. 26 and 27)
- questionnaire design and implementation (pp. 32 and 33)
- nearest-neighbour analysis (pp. 52 and 53)
- bipolar analysis (pp. 56 and 57)
- flow-line maps (desire lines) (pp. 76 and 77).

ONLINE TEST

Test yourself on sphere-of-influence maps at www.brightredbooks.net

ISOLINE MAPS

DON'T FORGET 

Refer to the detailed information on pp. 64 and 65 for the equipment needed to draw isoline maps.

PURPOSE

Isoline maps show lines that join points of equal value. You will already be familiar with this type of map – for example, the contours on an OS map, isotherms of temperature and isobars of pressure. Isolines can only be used when the data (variables) to be plotted change gradually in space and where sufficient data have been gathered.

Europe: Total precipitation in mm, 11–17 May 2014

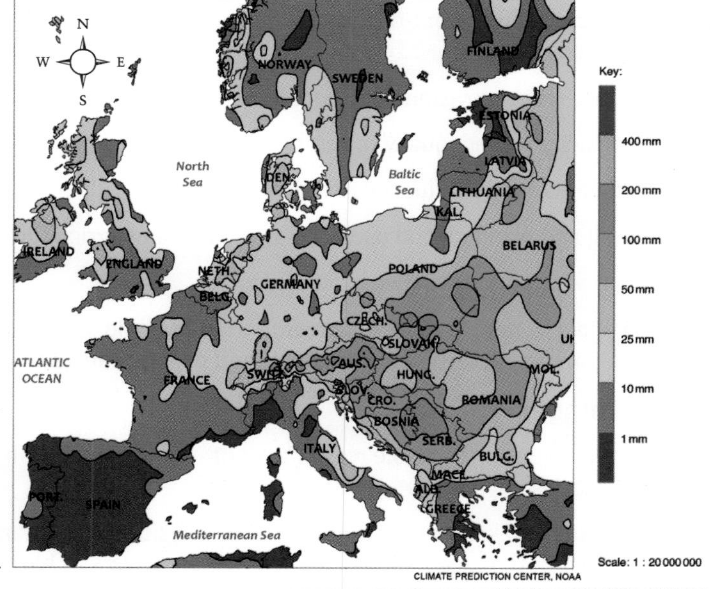

Example of an isoline map.

ONLINE 

Check out the link on the Digital Zone to see a list of 34 different isoline maps.

CONSTRUCTING AN ISOLINE MAP

The important features of isoline maps are:

- isolines connect points of equal value
- the isolines do not cross or touch (with the exception of vertical gradients, such as cliffs)
- the **interval** is the numerical difference between adjacent isolines and is usually the same over the entire map
- isolines pass between higher and lower values.

Follow these steps to construct an isoline map:

- plot the gathered data on a base map as a series of points with accompanying values
- decide the interval you want between the isolines – a small interval means many isolines, whereas large intervals may generalise the data
- draw the isolines following the advice given here and in the video
- the space between different value isolines can be shaded or coloured – use darker shading/colours for higher values
- add a key, title, scale, compass direction and data source to the map.

VIDEO LINK 

See how to draw an isoline map by watching the clip at www.brightredbooks.net

ANALYSING AN ISOLINE MAP

When analysing isoline maps, you should be able to explain, within the context of the question/data, the spatial patterns illustrated in the mapped data with reference to relevant background geographical knowledge and understanding. Any anomalous results should be explained by referring to other sources or research.

To fully appreciate the displayed data, always consider the nature of the construction of the map and use an atlas to obtain a wider perspective, taking into account that:

contd

VIDEO LINK 

Watch the video at www.brightredbooks.net to learn how to analyse isoline maps.

- if you need to work out the value of a certain point on a map, you have to follow one of the isolines until you reach the value written on the line
- smaller isolines do not always have values written on them, so you need to read the value of a more important isoline (shown as a bold line) and then deduce the value of the smaller isoline
- isolines show gradients – that is, the amount of change over a certain distance
- isolines closer together represent a high gradient, whereas isolines far apart represent a low gradient
- in nature, gradients usually indicate a flow from higher values towards lower values (e.g. air moving from an area of high pressure to an area of low pressure)
- steep gradients usually indicate a faster flow – for example, water flowing down a mountain side.

CONSIDERATIONS/LIMITATIONS OF ISOLINE MAPS

Advantages

- show gradual changes and patterns over large spatial areas
- isolines join places of equal value along their length
- use fixed intervals so changes can be easily identified
- can add colour/density shading to enhance patterns/trends
- can be superimposed onto a base map
- easily drawn using computer software packages
- can show areas of equal value
- avoid the problem of boundary lines.

Disadvantages

- there may be variations in the location of each isoline
- shading implies equal values between the isolines
- requires data for a large number of locations
- does not show discontinuous distributions
- only work where there is plenty of data spread over the study area and the changes are gradual
- small lines and numbers on graphs can be difficult to read.

ONLINE

Follow the link on the Digital Zone for the Geographical Base Map Library.

ONLINE

Follow the links at www.brightredbooks.net to sites that provide good information, examples and tests for isoline maps.

ONLINE

Check out the Geographical Association Base Maps Library link at www.brightredbooks.net

DON'T FORGET

Isoline maps show elements that vary continuously over an area, rather than point values, categories or uniform areas.

ONLINE TEST

Head to www.brightredbooks.net to test yourself on isoline maps.

THINGS TO DO AND THINK ABOUT

Refer to the generic advice for graphs on pp. 64 and 65 and the following specific points.

Think about the possible links that isoline maps have with other geographical techniques in this study guide.

Watch the video on how to add velocity data to a river cross-section, and find more examples of isoline maps on the Digital Zone.

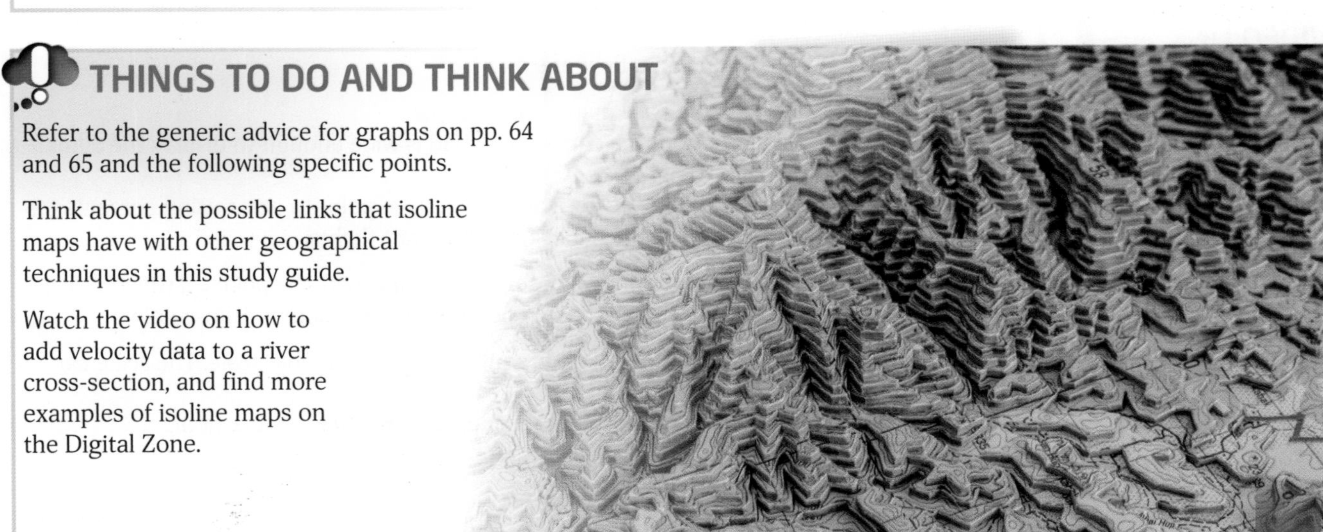

FLOW-LINE MAPS

DON'T FORGET

Refer to the detailed information on pp. 64 and 65 for the equipment needed to draw a flow-line map.

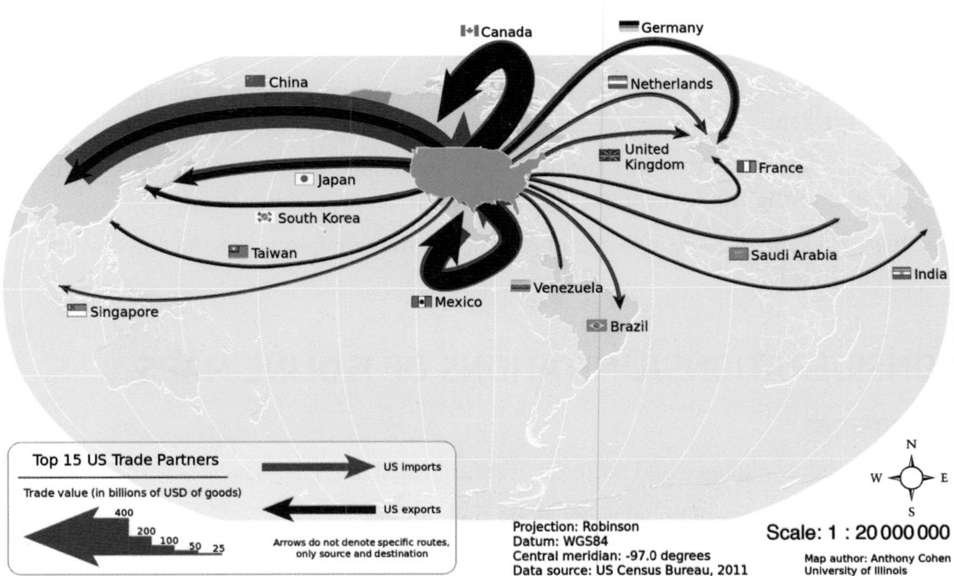

Flow-line map – example A.

ONLINE

Read the article at www.brightredbooks.net to find out more about flow-line maps.

PURPOSE

Flow-lines are used on a map to show the actual flow and direction of movement – for example, in a traffic-flow map, a line is drawn along the road and is proportional in width to the volume of the traffic flow. The flow-line is drawn proportional to the actual number of vehicles moving along the route using an appropriate scale. The width of the line represents the rate of flow, and the arrow represents the direction of flow.

Flow-line maps can be used to show:

- migration routes
- river discharge
- traffic flows.

VIDEO LINK

See how to draw a flow-line map by watching the clip at www.brightredbooks.net

CONSTRUCTING A FLOW-LINE MAP

The important issues in constructing flow-line maps are:

- keeping the background information as simple as possible to avoid clutter
- choosing an appropriate scale so that extreme values can be shown
- providing a key.

Follow these steps to construct a flow-line map:

1. Draw or access a suitable base map – for example:
   - a large-scale map where the course of a road is wide enough to display the actual/raw data
   - a small-scale map where the lines are drawn from point to point using percentages or square-root values of the data, such as aircraft flights.

If the map is to represent flows along an observed network, mark the points at which vehicles were observed, where you stood and the number of vehicles counted at those points.

2. Review the range of the gathered data, and decide on a suitable scale. The scale can be based on:
   - the raw data or actual values – for example, 1 mm = 100 cars per hour, 2 mm = 200 cars per hour

contd

- percentage values for the data – for example, the percentage total migration from one location to another, which is good for comparing flows in opposite directions
- the square root of the data values – use this value when the flow-lines are too wide and are likely to obscure the map.

3. Draw the lines:
   - from the origin to the destination (see example A)
   - along the actual route (see example B).

You can include two-way movement – such as exports/imports – by using different shading.

4. Add a key/legend, title, scale, compass direction and data source to the map.

ANALYSING A FLOW-LINE MAP

When analysing flow-line maps, you should be able to explain, within the context of the question/data, the spatial patterns illustrated in the mapped data with reference to relevant background geographical knowledge and understanding. Any anomalous results should be explained by referring to other sources or research.

To fully appreciate the displayed data, always consider the nature of the map's construction and use an atlas to obtain a wider perspective, remembering that:

- you need to take particular care when reading the key/legend
- the scale of the map may be based on raw data, percentages or the square root of the data
- the width of the line is important, not the length
- if the lines are proportional in value, then a value twice as high needs a line of double the width
- although the map is good for showing 'big and small' and giving an idea of where events are concentrated, it is less effective for comparison across a range because it is difficult for the human eye to interpret the relative size of two-dimensional objects (although a good key will help).

CONSIDERATIONS/LIMITATIONS OF FLOW-LINE MAPS

Advantages

- show movement of people, goods and transport
- show volume and direction of movement
- scale/width of lines proportional to value
- can be superimposed onto a base map
- immediate visual impression
- clear location component.

Disadvantages

- hard to draw
- flows can be in the same direction/overlap
- may be difficult to show the meeting point of wide bands without overwhelming the map
- the real distance and direction may have been distorted to achieve a clearer image.

THINGS TO DO AND THINK ABOUT

Refer to the generic advice for graphs on pp. 64 and 65 and the following specific points.

Think about the possible links that flow-line maps have with other geographical techniques in this study guide.

You may also see references in textbooks and online to desire lines and trip lines. These are variations of flow-lines that are used in geography for specific purposes. For more details about these forms, see the Digital Zone.

ONLINE

Follow the link on the Digital Zone for the Geographical Base Map Library.

ONLINE

Check out the Geographical Association Base Maps Library link at www.brightredbooks.net

ONLINE TEST

Head to www.brightredbooks.net to test yourself on flow-line maps.

CROSS-SECTIONS

DON'T FORGET

Refer to the detailed information on pp. 64 and 65 for the equipment needed to draw a cross-section.

PURPOSE

A cross-section is a profile (side view) of the area being researched. Cross-sections are used to show changes in relief (shape and height or depth) along a line drawn between two points.

Cross-sections can be used to show the shape of:

- a slope surveyed using the methods outlined on pp. 10 and 11 (beach-profile analysis) and pp. 16 and 17 (slope analysis)
- a river channel at a single point (pp. 20 and 21, stream analysis) or to compare the shape of a river channel at different points
- a valley at a single point or to compare the shape of a valley at different points, such as investigating valley features created by ice
- a long profile of a river showing gradient changes as it flows downstream – ranging poles are positioned at equal distances upstream and downstream of the cross-section sites (these can be fairly far apart and still easily visible), and the slope angle is found using a clinometer (pp. 10 and 11, beach profile; pp. 20 and 21, stream analysis); the results can be related to information on velocity, bedload/sediment and efficiency.

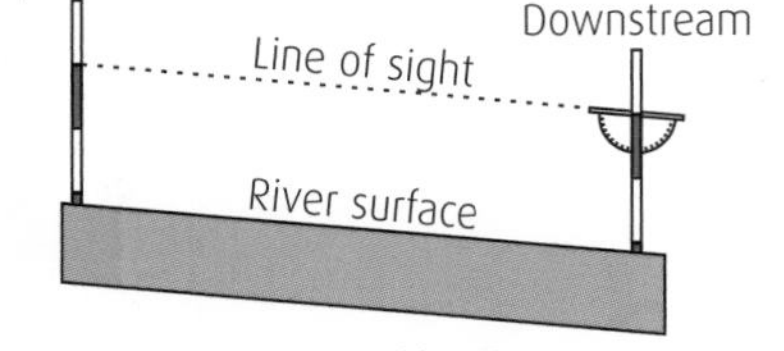

Measuring the profile of a river.

CONSTRUCTING A CROSS-SECTION

Method 1: drawing a cross-section using an OS map

Stage 1:

1. Decide the line of the cross-section – that is, the start and end points:
   - to draw the shape of a river valley, the line is best drawn at right angles to the river and connecting the highest points on either side of the valley
   - to draw the shape of a landscape, the line is best drawn where the lowest and highest points can be shown.

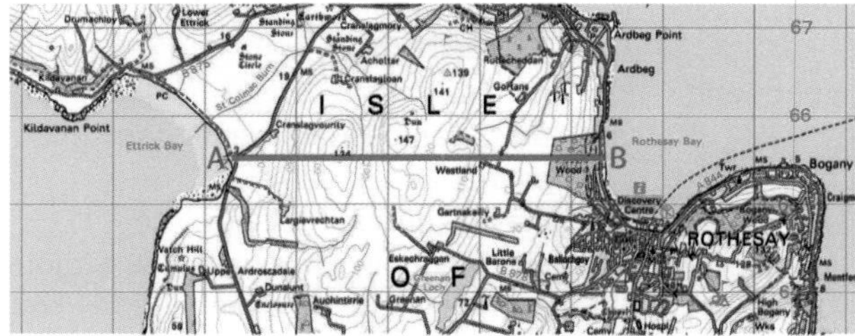

Cross-section from Ettrick Bay (043656) to Rothesay Bay (084656), Isle of Bute.

2. Draw a pencil line lightly between the start and end points on the OS map.
3. Use a straight-edged piece of paper and place it along the line of the cross-section on the map.
4. Mark the beginning and end of the cross-section and write down the grid references.

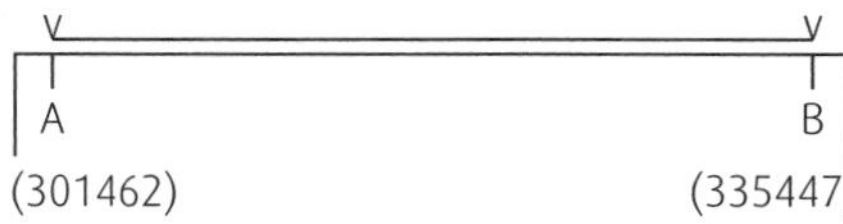

5. Move along the line of the cross-section, making a mark every time a contour line passes under the edge of the paper. Add height numbers following this advice:
   - if you don't have a number for a particular line, count up or down from one you do have
   - look out for places where the same contour line crosses the paper more than once
   - remember there is a gap of 10 m between contour lines, 100 and 50 m lines are shown in bold and the tops of the height numbers are towards the top of the slope.

VIDEO LINK

See how to draw a cross-section by watching the clip at www.brightredbooks.net

ONLINE

See how to draw a cross-section by following the link at www.brightredbooks.net

ONLINE TEST

Head to www.brightredbooks.net to test yourself on cross-sections.

contd

6. Mark the position of any main features, such as rivers or roads. The more detail you collect at this point the better, but be careful not to over-clutter the paper.

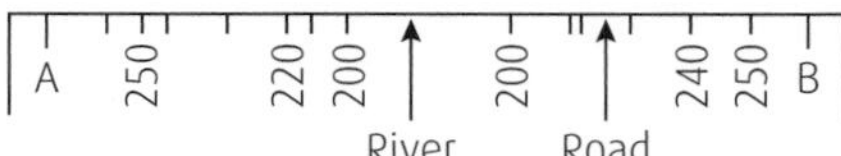

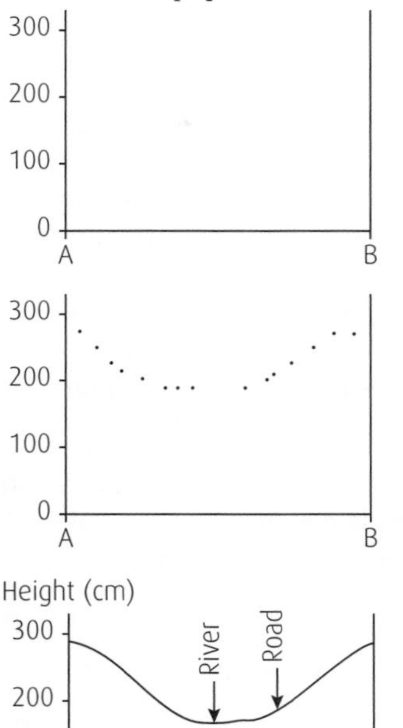

Stage 2:

1. On graph paper, draw a frame for your cross-section:
   - the length along the bottom should be the same as your cross-section line
   - the scale on the side axis should be in 10 m intervals up to the maximum height in your cross-section.
2. Place your piece of paper along the bottom of the frame and carefully mark a dot in the correct place for each contour line (see video on the Digital Zone for technique).
3. Join the dots with a smooth line and check back to the map to make sure your cross-section looks sensible.
4. Annotate the cross-section to highlight important features, such as the river or steep valley sides.
5. Ensure the cross-section has a key, title, scale and the grid references of the start and end points.

Method 2: Drawing the cross-section of a river channel

See pp. 20 and 21 (stream analysis) and the information on the Digital Zone for the full methodology.

Vertical exaggeration

When you check the final cross-section, it may look distorted. It can appear much steeper, narrower and higher than in reality. The vertical exaggeration shows how much the vertical scale has been distorted. Five times is a relatively good representation; an exaggeration larger than five times becomes too distorted. The vertical scale chosen will therefore have a huge effect on the distortion of the cross-section.

Example:

1 cm represents 20 m
1 cm represents 20 m × 100 (there are 100 cm in 1 m)
1 cm represents 2000 cm
Scale = 1:2000

Now the vertical scale is in the same format as the horizontal scale (e.g. 1:50 000).

Use the following formula to calculate the vertical exaggeration:

$$\text{Vertical exaggeration} = \frac{\text{horizontal scale}}{\text{vertical scale}} = \frac{50\,000}{2000} = 25 \text{ times.}$$

DON'T FORGET

Cross-sections need to be used appropriately to show gathered data.

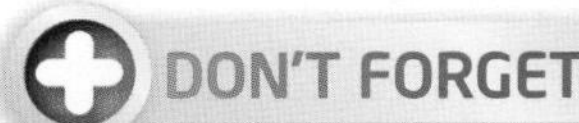

DON'T FORGET

Care has to be taken when adding annotations to a cross-section so as not to clutter the diagram or confuse the message being displayed.

ONLINE

Use the Geographical Association Base Maps Library link at www.brightredbooks.net

VIDEO LINK

Watch the video at www.brightredbooks.net for an explanation of vertical exaggeration.

THINGS TO DO AND THINK ABOUT

Refer to the generic advice for graphs on pp. 64 and 65 and the following specific point.

Think about the possible links that cross-sections have with other geographical techniques in this study guide.

Use the links on the Digital Zone to see how to draw a geological cross-section.

TRANSECTS

PURPOSE

A transect is a (usually) straight line that joins any two points on a map. Transects can show features of both physical and human environments and how they change from place to place. They can also be used to show relationships between physical and human factors that may be responsible for the observed changes along a transect. Sometimes they are drawn to represent changes over very small areas and represent different land uses resulting from changes in relief, soil, aspect, environmental quality, socio-economic activity or land value.

A transect can be used to illustrate data gathered from a number of the techniques explained in this study guide. Refer to the specific techniques for more detail on how to carry out a transect survey to investigate changes:

- along and across a beach (pp. 10 and 11, beach profile)
- on a slope (pp. 16 and 17, slope analysis)
- in soil profiles pp. 18 and 19, soil analysis)
- in vegetation (pp. 22 and 23, vegetation analysis)
- environmental quality (pp. 24 and 25, environmental-quality survey)
- in pedestrian and traffic flows (pp. 28 and 29, pedestrian/traffic survey)
- across a rural landscape (pp. 34 and 35, rural land-use mapping)
- across an urban landscape (pp. 36 and 37, urban land-use mapping).

DON'T FORGET 

Refer to the detailed information on pp. 64 and 65 for the equipment needed to construct a transect.

VIDEO LINK 

Watch the video at www.brightredbooks.net for information about using transects.

ONLINE 

Head to www.brightredbooks.net to see examples of various transects.

VIDEO LINK 

Check out the video on constructing a transact of a topographic map at www.brightredbooks.net

CONSTRUCTING A TRANSECT

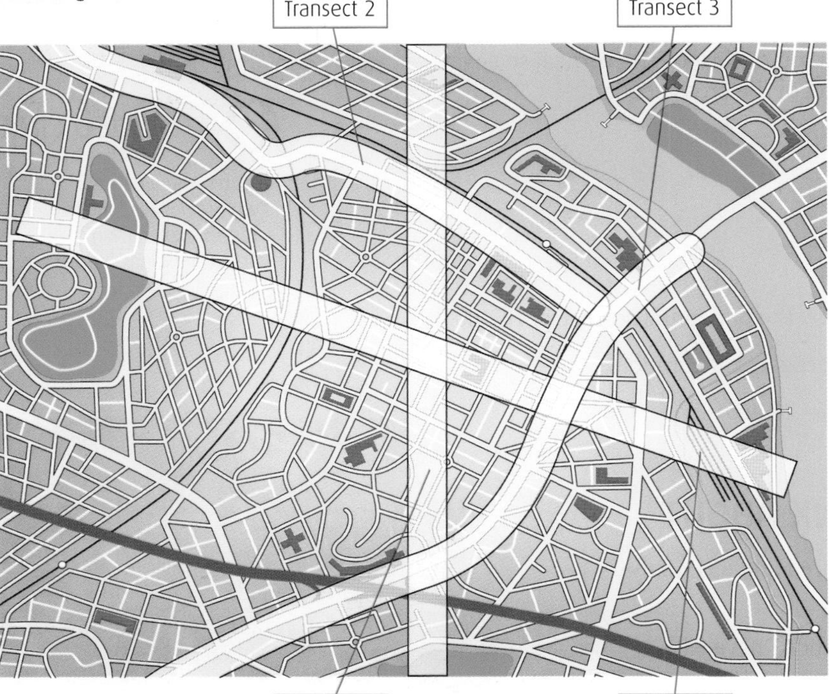

Example of several transects in one area.

There are several ways of displaying data collected along a transect:

- a line graph for continuous data
- a scatter graph when the data is not continuous
- a pictogram could be a good visual display of relevant data
- cross-sections can be used as a base with superimposed graphs, such as line graphs, bar graphs and pie charts
- the transect map can be coloured or shaded to illustrate features along the transect, such as land use, building age/height, vegetation and soil type
- a completed transect map/diagram can also include additional information above/below the line of the transect.

It may be possible to combine several transects to produce a more complete picture of the surveyed landscape, such as along a beach or out from a central point (e.g. the central business district).

contd

ANALYSING A CROSS-SECTION OR A TRANSECT

When analysing a cross-section or a transect, you should be able to explain, within the context of the question/data, the spatial patterns illustrated in the mapped data with reference to relevant background geographical knowledge and understanding. Any anomalous results should be explained by referring to other sources or research.

To fully appreciate the displayed data, refer back to the source data, the OS map or an atlas to obtain a wider perspective and to take into account:

for cross-sections:

- the angle of the slope
- the vertical exaggeration
- the scale – vertical height or depth.

for both cross-sections and transects:

- the annotations on or around the diagram
- the nature of their construction.

CONSIDERATIONS/LIMITATIONS OF A CROSS-SECTION OR TRANSECT

Advantages

- they provide a good visual overview of the survey area
- they can show a view of a section of a river/valley or part of a rural/urban landscape
- they can be compared with other cross-sections or transects
- several transects from a central point can be compared.

Disadvantages

- a single cross-section has limited value – it is more useful to compare cross-sections/long profiles
- incorrect or exaggerated vertical scales on a cross-section can be misleading
- they are only a snapshot in time
- they take time to draw and need to be an accurate representation of reality.

THINGS TO DO AND THINK ABOUT

Refer to the generic advice for graphs on pp. 64 and 65 and the following specific points.

Think about the possible links that transects have with other geographical techniques in this study guide.

See pp. 58 and 59 for how to use a kite diagram to illustrate vegetation along a transect.

DON'T FORGET

Transects need to be used appropriately to show gathered data.

DON'T FORGET

Care has to be taken when adding annotations to transects so as not to clutter the diagram or confuse the message being displayed.

ONLINE

Use the Geographical Association Base Maps Library link at www.brightredbooks.net

ONLINE TEST

Head to www.brightredbooks.net to test yourself on and see examples of transects.

VIDEO LINK

Watch the videos on distribution at www.brightredbooks.net

PROJECT FOLIO

GENERAL ADVICE ON THE PROJECT FOLIO

PURPOSE OF THE PROJECT

'The purpose of this project folio is to demonstrate challenge and application by requiring the candidate to draw on and apply skills, knowledge and understanding within the context of research relating to a geographical study and issue. This may be related to areas candidates have studied in class if they wish, but they are free to research any appropriate geographical study and issue.'

Source: SQA Advanced Higher Geography Project folio General Assessment Information

The project folio will allow you to develop your independent research skills by:

- identifying an appropriate complex topic for the study and/or an issue to research
- planning a programme of research
- researching, collecting and recording information
- evaluating, synthesising and analysing information or evidence
- understanding approaches to organising, presenting and referencing findings in an appropriate geographical style.

ONLINE 

Check out the following resources at www.brightredbooks.net

- geographical-study flow diagram
- glossary of terms
- ideas for a potential topic
- IB Geography ten-step plan
- Harvard guide to using sources

WHAT YOU NEED TO KNOW

Before continuing, go to pp. 4–7 in this guide and read all the information and advice again.

The advice and guidance contained within the following pages will assume that:

- you want to achieve the maximum number of marks allocated for each of the criteria
- you have acquired the relevant geographical skills and techniques outlined in the pages of this study guide and can apply those skills and techniques appropriately within the context of your chosen geographical study and geographical issue
- you have access to, have read thoroughly and will refer to the advice and guidance in the following SQA documentation:
  - Advanced Higher Geography Course Assessment Specification (C733 77) http://www.sqa.org.uk/files_ccc/AHCASGeography.pdf
  - General Assessment Information for Advanced Higher Geography http://www.sqa.org.uk/files_ccc/GAInfoAHGeography.pdf
  - Guidance on Conditions of Assessment for Coursework http://www.sqa.org.uk/sqa/files_ccc/Guidance_on_conditions_of_assessment_for_coursework.pdf
  - Advanced Higher Geography Course/Unit Support Notes http://www.sqa.org.uk/files_ccc/AHCUSNGeography.pdf
  - Advanced Higher Geography Project folio Assessment Task
    This document is kept on the SQA secure website. Ask your teacher/lecturer for a printout of this resource because it was designed to be shared with candidates as part of the Advanced Higher Geography learning experience.
  - Verification and Course Reports – useful guidance and advice based on actual candidate responses in a particular year http://www.sqa.org.uk/sqa/48465.html
  - SQA Understanding Standards – Exemplification of Candidate Responses and Mark Allocation – designed for teachers and markers, but also of use to candidates http://www.understandingstandards.org.uk/Subjects/Geography/advanced/source

ONLINE 

Find links to these documents listed at www.brightredbooks.net

Carrying out an urban land-use survey.

DON'T FORGET 

If the word count for the geographical study exceeds the maximum by 10%, then a penalty may be applied.

FORMAT OF THE PROJECT FOLIO

The project folio consists of two parts: the geographical study and the geographical issue.

contd

Section A: geographical study (60 marks)

To be successful, you will need to:
A. justify the choice of a complex geographical topic to research (4 marks)
B. plan and carry out detailed research, which could include fieldwork (10 marks)
C. evaluate the research techniques and reliability of the data gathered (8 marks)
D. demonstrate a detailed knowledge and understanding of the topic being studied from wider reading (8 marks)
E. use a wide range of appropriate techniques to process the gathered information (10 marks)
F. analyse all the information that has been gathered and processed to identify and explain relationships (12 marks)
G. reach reasoned conclusion(s) supported by a wide range of evidence (8 marks).

The completed geographical study should be no more than 3000 words in length (excluding any text used on the front covers, in the list of contents, any annotations to illustrations, the references, the bibliography and the appendices). The word count must be submitted by the candidate with the completed project folio (study).

Refer to pp. 8–37 (data-gathering techniques) and pp. 38–82 (data-processing techniques).

Section B: geographical Issue (40 marks)

To be successful, you will need to:
A. justify the choice of a current complex geographical issue to critically evaluate (4 marks)
B. undertake wider background reading from a wide range of sources relating to the geographical issue (8 marks)
C. summarise a wide range of viewpoints on the complex geographical issue (10 marks)
D. critically evaluate each of the viewpoints (10 marks)
E. reach a reasoned conclusion supported by a wide range of evidence (8 marks).

The completed geographical issue should be no more than 1800 words in length (excluding any text used on the front covers, in the list of contents, any annotations to illustrations, the references, the bibliography and the appendices). The word count must be submitted by the candidate with the completed project folio (issue).

See the listed web links to assist you with your critical evaluation.

You need to respond to all the criteria in both the geographical study (criteria A–G) and the geographical issue (criteria A–E). However, the starting point is not choosing/justifying a title (criterion A), but rather to begin by doing some research/background/wider reading (study – criteria B and D; issue – criterion B) to develop ideas about which topic/issue you might choose.

LAYOUT OF THE PROJECT

A critical skill is to understand how your findings should be presented in such a way as to be clear and reliable and to reflect a relevant geographical style. There is no single way to achieve this; and you should consider different possible approaches to organising and referencing your work.

WORKING WITH OTHERS

It might be helpful to work with others for some of the time when you are researching your study or issue – for example, when carrying out fieldwork. Any group fieldwork should be acknowledged in your study. It is important that the evidence you produce is your own work.

THINGS TO DO AND THINK ABOUT

The links on the Digital Zone will take you to useful academic resources providing general help, details of how to undertake a critical evaluation and essay-writing advice.

Think about the connections between the criteria in the study and the issue.

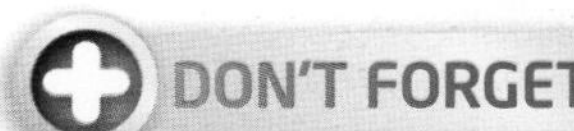

If the word count for the geographical issues essay exceeds the maximum by 10%, then a penalty may be applied.

Evaluate your responses as you progress through the study and the issue.

ONLINE

Check out the following resources at www.brightredbooks.net

ONLINE

For detailed advice, refer to the Advanced Higher Geography Course/Unit Support Notes, pp. 38–40, bullet point 5. Find the link at www.brightredbooks.net

ONLINE

Check out the resources at www.brightredbooks.net.

GEOGRAPHICAL STUDY 1

ONLINE 

Check out the following resources at www.brightredbooks.net

- geographical-study flow diagram
- glossary of terms
- ideas for a potential topic
- IB Geography ten-step plan
- Harvard guide to using sources

ONLINE 

Check out ideas and suggestions for research at www.brightredbooks.net

DON'T FORGET 

To complete criterion A, you will have had to consider and have acted on criteria B and D.

CRITERION A

Justify the choice of a complex geographical topic to research (4 marks).

You should choose a topic that will allow you to:

- carry out wide-ranging research using both primary and secondary sources, where appropriate, to gather relevant data, related to the research question
- summarise and process geographical data/information
- analyse and evaluate geographical data/information
- reach reasoned conclusions.

To maximise your marks, you should justify your choice of topic in terms of:

- the purpose of researching the topic – that is, why your topic is worth learning about
- the geographical relevance of the topic – that is, why this topic is important to geography
- any relevant geographical literature/research that you can refer to, such as acknowledged research/theory
- what areas of analysis/evaluation your topic will involve – that is, how you are going to explain or reason the topic
- what geographical data/information of your topic you will process – that is, what are you going to do with the data collected.

The evidence for these points does not necessarily need to be stated at the beginning of the study. Credit will be given wherever these points are appropriately covered within the body of the study.

Providing details means that you include specific evidence and examples from geographical literature/research that you have found through your wider reading/research.

If your justification is weak, then it sets a weak premise for the study. Be clear and precise about the who, where, what, why and how of the study.

CRITERION B

Plan and carry out detailed research, which could include fieldwork (10 marks).

You should:

- carry out extensive background reading on the topic you have chosen (you should aim to use three or more sources of information)
- aim to generate four or more research questions/hypotheses or sub-questions/hypotheses related to the overall aim of your study, and organise them logically
- identify appropriate sampling techniques and sampling points for the gathering of data
- identify the appropriate data-gathering methods, techniques and equipment.

To maximise your marks, there should be clear evidence of highly detailed planning for research, which will include:

- at least four complex research questions/hypotheses or sub-questions/hypotheses, the relevance of which you can support by referring to three relevant sources of information – that is, referring to geographical theory or guides on how to carry out a specific research technique, such as an urban land-use survey
- the use of research (-gathering) techniques appropriate to your choice of topic that (a) have been used with an evident high degree of skill and (b) will allow the research questions to be explained in detail or hypotheses to be skilfully tested – that is, the evidence within the study shows/explains the methodology used and assures the marker that you have gathered sufficient and suitable information on which to proceed to process and analyse data.

You should have thought out and be able to show the connections between:

- your choice of topic
- the questions/hypothesis researched
- how you went about gathering the appropriate information – that is, using the correct research/data-gathering techniques in the right context, such as a transect across a beach
- developed methods to acquire the right information, such as interviews and questionnaires

contd

- acquired sufficient data to respond to the research question/hypothesis.

Fieldwork will be an important part of the project folio (study) in many cases. However, you do not need to carry out fieldwork if other research methods will give you the information you need. You can still gain full marks without carrying out any fieldwork.

The evidence for these bulleted points does not need to be at a specific point in the study. Credit will be given where these points are evidenced appropriately within the body of the study.

Research techniques refer to gathering data from primary and secondary sources.

DON'T FORGET

To finally complete criterion B, you will have had to have considered and acted on criterion D – that is, wider reading on a range of techniques for your chosen topic.

CRITERION C

Evaluate the research techniques and the reliability of data gathered (8 marks).

Evaluation involves making reasoned comments relating to, for example:

- the relevance/importance/reliability of gathered data
- the positive and negative aspects of techniques used
- the strengths and weaknesses of techniques used
- the significance/impact of data gathered
- any other relevant evaluative comments.

Warning: this section is not about discussing your research experience. This is the point at which you need to take a step back, before proceeding to processing and analysing your gathered data, and consider carefully whether you have:

- a topic worthy of research
- developed the right questions/hypothesis to fit the topic and research methodology
- used the correct data-gathering techniques for the chosen topic
- demonstrated your ability to carry out techniques in a way that has allowed you to gather credible and reliable data
- considered the issues/problems encountered during the gathering process and dealt with them to resolve the issue/problem – for example, refined the research questions and carried out further research.

To maximise your marks, you should:

- evaluate the data-gathering techniques used by assessing the quality of the data obtained and comparing these with estimates where appropriate – for example, does the gathering technique look as if it is appropriate as expected/as per a referenced theory/supporting evidence from secondary research/wider reading?
- evaluate the reliability of the data with reference to sampling techniques and the number of samples – for example, have you used the correct methodology/sampling technique(s) to gather credible and reliable data, and will the data gathered be sufficient/suitable to proceed.
- evaluate the significance of the data – for example, does the data collected support your expectations, and, if not, why not?
- explain and analyse the next steps you might take – for example, do you need to:
  - reconsider the research technique(s)used
  - amend the methodology, such as the sampling technique
  - undertake further fieldwork/research
  - do further reading/collect secondary data.

DON'T FORGET

Always amend/update your research questions as required.

Make a plan.

DON'T FORGET

To finally complete criterion C, you will have had to have considered and acted on criteria A, B and D.

THINGS TO DO AND THINK ABOUT

Don't proceed to processing your gathered data until you are sure you have sufficient reliable and credible data.

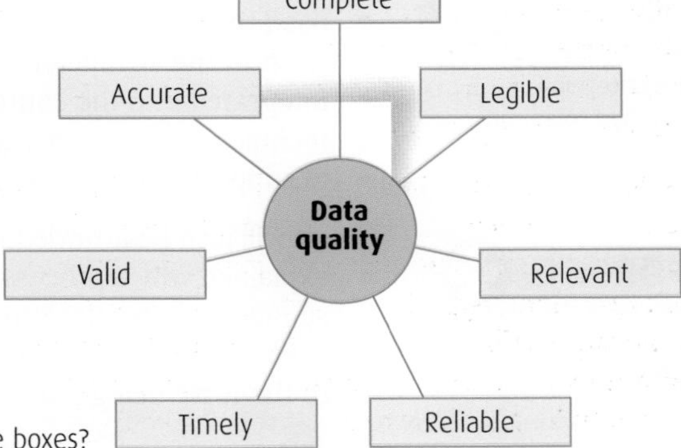
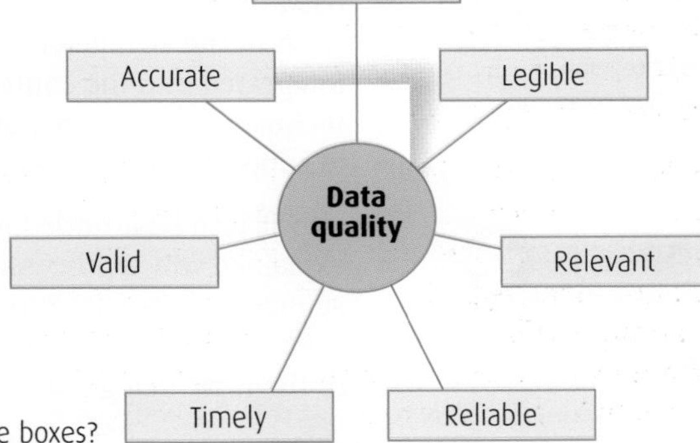

Does your data tick all these boxes?

GEOGRAPHICAL STUDY 2

CRITERION D

Demonstrate a detailed knowledge and understanding of the topic being studied from wider reading (8 marks).

You should use your knowledge and understanding within the context of the topic being studied, and support your response to the topic.

To maximise your marks you should include, at the appropriate point(s) within the study, at least three points of evidence from wider reading that are:

- relevant to the topic being studied
- developed (by including additional detail, exemplification, reasons or related evidence, integrating the knowledge and understanding of this evidence as further support for your line of argument)
- used to support the findings from research relevant to the topic being studied
- using the knowledge and understanding as evidence to provide further in-depth evaluation/analysis.

This is the opportunity to show the marker that you have read widely around the theme of your topic. You should make reference to acknowledged research/theory to support the evidence you have gathered in the processing of that evidence, the analysis and the conclusion reached.

CRITERION E

Use a wide range of appropriate techniques to process the gathered information (10 marks).

You should aim to:

- use three or more different processing techniques (e.g. graphical or statistical) to support your research
- explain how and why you have used these processing techniques
- ensure that your choice of techniques is relevant to the hypotheses/sub-aims/ research questions
- suggest potential improvements or adjustments
- make sure the techniques selected are sophisticated (appropriate to the chosen topic of study) and clearly able to show relationships between the relevant data.

To maximise your marks, you should include, at the appropriate point(s) within the study, at least three different processing techniques (e.g. statistical, graphical or mapping) which are:

- relevant to the topic being studied – for example, mapping using a sphere-of-influence map
- used to process gathered information appropriately – for example, statistical testing to show the significance of your results
- integrated into the context/argument of the study – for example, graphical techniques such as a scatter graph
- in support of the research – for example, mapping using a transect.

Credit will also be awarded where you have:

- explained why a processing technique is relevant to the topic
- suggested potential improvements or adjustments that could be or were made
- used additional processing techniques skilfully, which were appropriate and relevant to the topic being studied.

DON'T FORGET 

You should include clear references to all sources you have used within a detailed bibliography.

ONLINE 

For detailed advice, refer to the Advanced Higher Geography Course/Unit Support Notes, pp.38–40, bullet point 5. Find the link at www.brightredbooks.net

DON'T FORGET 

To complete criterion D, you will have had to show your use of this criterion throughout the whole process.

ONLINE 

For detailed advice, refer to the Advanced Higher Geography Course/Unit Support Notes, pp. 38–40, bullet point 5. Find the link at www.brightredbooks.net

DON'T FORGET 

It is not the number of techniques that is important, but their relevance and sophistication.

DON'T FORGET 

To complete criterion E, you will have had to act on criteria A–D.

DON'T FORGET 

Use the latest versions of SQA documents.

CRITERION F

Analyse all the information that has been gathered and processed to identify and explain relationships (12 marks).

Analysis involves using the relevant data to identify and explain links/relationships within the wider context of the study.

To maximise your marks you should include, at the appropriate point(s) within the study, at least four analytical statements that refer to:

- the links/relationships between the different data sets that have been gathered and processed – for example, pebble size and location
- the links/relationships between the different data sets and the wider context of the study – for example, how the results/findings fit into the bigger picture
- the links/relationships between the data sets, the wider context and the related theories – for example, acknowledged research/ theory
- the similarities or contradictions between the data sets and related theories – for example, the integration of others' ideas/arguments/evidence with your own
- the possible consequences/implications of similarities or contradictions between the data sets analysed and related theories – for example, why your results do/don't fit the model/theory.

CRITERION G

Reach reasoned conclusion(s) supported by a wide range of evidence (8 marks).

You should use the different pieces of information to support your response to the questions raised in the topic. These can come from the sources you have researched and/ or your own knowledge.

You should organise your overall response into a logical sequence in response to the questions raised in the topic.

To maximise your marks you should include a conclusion(s) that presents an overall judgement about the topic.

The conclusion(s) should:

- be based on an examination of most or all **of** the gathered and processed information/research questions
- be supported by organising, linking and/or sequencing of ideas and based on relevant and accurate use of most/all of the information or evidence
- be based on the points developed within your argument – that is, linked to relevant analytical points supported by information or evidence
- make reference to evidence that supports your conclusion(s) – for example, quoting and/or using footnotes to reference acknowledged geographical research and theories
- if appropriate, make reference to potential challenges or counter-arguments to your conclusion(s) – that is, acknowledging there might be opposing research/theories.

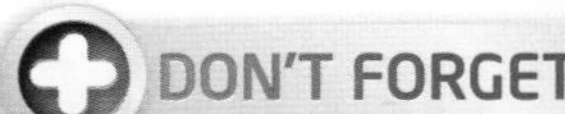

DON'T FORGET

You should aim to use your analysis to show that you understand the wider context of the topic being studied and/or relevant theoretical ideas.

DON'T FORGET

To complete criterion F, you will have had to have considered and acted on criteria A–E.

DON'T FORGET

Don't make your research fit into a prescribed or pre-determined solution or response.

DON'T FORGET

Always recognise anomalies and try to explain the reason for their existence.

DON'T FORGET

Your conclusion(s) can, but do(es) not have to, be made at the end.

DON'T FORGET

To complete criterion G, you will have had to have considered and acted on criteria A–F.

THINGS TO DO AND THINK ABOUT

Layout of the project:

A critical skill is to understand how your findings should be presented in such a way as to be clear and reliable and reflect a relevant geographical style. There is no single way to achieve this, and you should consider different possible approaches to organising and referencing your work.

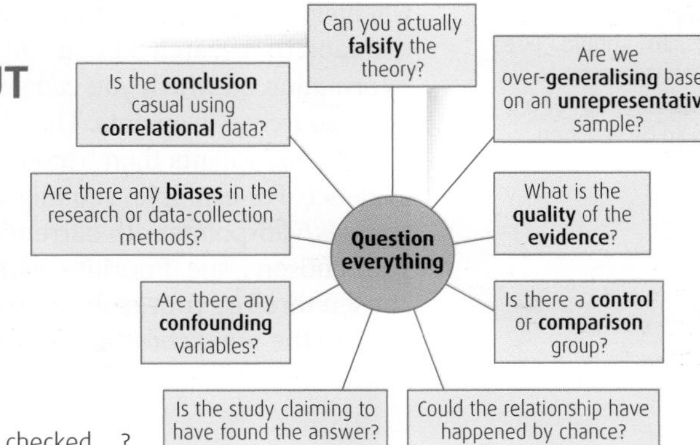

Have you checked ...?

COURSE ASSESSMENT

GEOGRAPHICAL ISSUE

ONLINE 

Check out the following resources at www.brightredbooks.net
- geographical-issue flow diagram
- glossary of terms
- ideas for a potential issue
- Harvard guide to using sources

ONLINE 

Check out ideas and suggestions for research at www.brightredbooks.net

DON'T FORGET 

To finally complete criterion A, you will have had to have considered and acted, to a degree, on criterion B – that is, wider background reading to choose an issue.

CRITERION A

Justify the choice of a current complex geographical issue to critically evaluate (4 marks).

You should choose a current geographical issue that will allow you to:
- carry out research relating to a wide range of sources with contrasting viewpoints
- use relevant additional detail
- summarise the viewpoints
- critically evaluate the sources/viewpoints.

To maximise your marks you should justify your choice of topic in terms of:
- the purpose of researching the issue – that is, why your issue is worth learning about
- the geographical relevance of the issue – that is, why this issue is important to geography
- any relevant geographical literature/research that you can refer to – for example, acknowledged research/theory
- what areas for evaluation your issue will involve – that is, how you are going to explain or reason the issue
- what geographical data/information your issue will/might involve you in processing – that is, what potential there is to process relevant data.

CRITERION B

Undertake wider background reading from a wide range of sources relating to the geographical issue (8 marks).

You should research at least three relevant sources, with a range of viewpoints, which are:
- up to date, where appropriate
- from peer-reviewed publications or written by experts in the field
- expressing views relevant to an issue
- listed correctly in a detailed bibliography.

To maximise your marks, you should:
- use three different sources of sufficient quality relevant to the issue
- use sources that contain sufficient detail and will be of sufficient length to be summarised
- have identified different perspectives/viewpoints on the complex geographical issue
- prioritise the sources for use in your response to the issue based on relevant criteria (e.g. the author's level of expertise).

To find three quality sources/viewpoints, you will have carried out a lot of wider reading. It is common to research an issue and find a wealth of information on which you can select/prioritise your three sources/viewpoints. The other peer-reviewed sources/viewpoints then become supporting evidence. For example: you might find six relevant sources/viewpoints with current information on your chosen issue. Prioritise, with valid reasons, your chosen three as your main sources/viewpoints and refer to the other three as supporting evidence.

DON'T FORGET 

The viewpoints could come to the same conclusion, but the arguments may be based on very different criteria.

DON'T FORGET 

Viewpoints need not be for or against your arguments, but should have sufficient controversy to allow evaluation and for a conclusion to be reached.

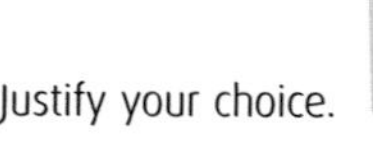

Justify your choice.

CRITERION C

Summarise a wide range of viewpoints on the complex geographical issue (10 marks).

Summarising involves identifying the key information within the viewpoints.

To maximise your marks you should:

- summarise three or more viewpoints effectively – that is, to demonstrate that you have a good understanding of the issue by going beyond its most obvious or familiar aspects
- organise your information systematically – that is, to be able to express, in detail, the key viewpoints proposed by the authors, including citations, and to include relevant maps/diagrams as an enhancement to the information where and as appropriate.

DON'T FORGET

Use the latest versions of SQA documents.

DON'T FORGET

Remember the purpose of summarising.

CRITERION D

Critically evaluate each of the viewpoints (10 marks).

You should aim to make reasoned, critically evaluative comments on the significance of the viewpoints.

Refer to the web links on pp. 82–83 to see how to undertake a critical evaluation.

To maximise your marks, you need to make explicit and critically perceptive evaluative comments on the significance of the viewpoints, which might include, where appropriate:

- assessing the credibility of the author and the publication
- assessing the quality of diagrams and statistics contained within sources
- identification of bias and/or exaggeration
- comparing and contrasting the viewpoints from a geographical perspective
- giving examples from wider reading to support your evaluative comments.

DON'T FORGET

Evaluation involves making a judgement based on criteria such as credibility and relevance.

DON'T FORGET

You must reach a conclusion on the issue rather than identifying your favoured source.

CRITERION E

Reach reasoned conclusion(s) supported by a wide range of evidence (8 marks).

You should give at least one conclusion that presents an overall judgement about the questions raised in the issue. It should be based on the points developed within your issue.

Your conclusion(s) can, but does not have to, be made at the end.

To maximise your marks, you should have a conclusion that:

- is well argued
- shows a clear understanding of the issue
- is well organised
- considers all the viewpoints you have researched
- is more than a repetition of information discussed earlier in the issue
- shows some insight
- is supported by organising, linking or sequencing of ideas using all the evidence.

DON'T FORGET

The conclusion need not be original, nor does it need to represent your personal view.

ONLINE

For detailed advice, refer to the Advanced Higher Geography Course/Unit Support Notes, pp. 38–40, bullet point 5. Find the link at www.brightredbooks.net

THINGS TO DO AND THINK ABOUT

A critical skill in laying out your project is to understand how your findings should be presented in such a way as to be clear and reliable and reflect a relevant geographical style. There is no single way to achieve this, and you should consider different possible approaches to organising and referencing your work.

QUESTION PAPER

STRUCTURE OF THE QUESTION PAPER

Every question has an answer.

PURPOSE

The question paper gives candidates an opportunity to demonstrate the following skills, knowledge and understanding:

- their knowledge of a wide range of geographical methods and techniques and understanding of the contexts in which they ought to be used
- the application of a wide range of geographical methods and techniques, including mapping skills, research/fieldwork skills, graphical techniques and statistical techniques for analysing and interpreting geographical data.

Know the question paper

The question paper will be marked out of 50 with questions or sub-questions from the three skill areas of the course, as follows.

- map interpretation (20 marks).
- data-gathering and processing techniques (10 marks).
- geographical data-handling (20 marks).

QUESTION-PAPER PACK

The Advanced Higher Geography question paper comes as a pack of materials that include the following items:

- the question paper

Question 1 – Map Interpretation

To answer this question you need to use:

- Supplementary Item A – Ordnance Survey (OS) Map, Extract No 1746/EXP189 1:25000 (Explorer Series), Hereford and the Wye Valley
- Supplementary Item B – Overlay 1
- Supplementary Item C – Overlay 2
- The atlas provided

You should make use of the whole map extract in your responses.

- supplementary items linked to the questions (the number of supplementary items may vary from year to year) – the relevant supplementary items for each question are listed under the question heading within the question paper (see Question 1, Specimen Question Paper)
- answer booklet.

You are allowed to use an appropriate, clean, unmarked atlas during the examination.

An atlas is a valuable resource and will help you locate the OS map extract in its broader setting and provide thematic information that can be included in your response to any question.

Before you start answering any questions, make sure you have all of these items.

ONLINE 

The SQA Advanced Higher Course Assessment Specification can be found at www.brightredbooks.net

General advice on answering questions

The following advice will help you to maximise your marks in the question paper:

- make sure you have pens, pencils, rubber, ruler and any other items you may need use during the examination
- you have 2 hours and 30 minutes to answer all the questions in the paper
- questions can be answered in any order
- questions within the paper may focus on one particular skill area, or they may integrate more than one skill area
- questions will require candidates to integrate geographical skills to explain, analyse and evaluate information and to structure a response
- questions will draw on the skills, knowledge and understanding described in the 'Further mandatory information on course coverage' section (see the SQA Advanced Higher Geography Course Assessment Specification, pp. 7 and 8)
- allocate sufficient time for each question – as a rough guide, you might allocate time based on the marks awarded for each question (e.g. Question 1, 1 hour; Question 2, 30 minutes; and Question 3, 1 hour)
- use a watch or wall clock to check the time during the examination

contd

- read through the information on the front cover of the question paper
- questions usually include some text-box information that has been included to set the context for the question and provide support (e.g. Question 1 b(i), Specimen Question Paper)

> Maps produced by the Environment Agency show that possible flood levels for the River Wye could affect areas up to the 50 metre contour. Supplementary Item C shows the River Wye and the 50 metre contour line.

- make sure you identify the command word in each question and answer the question accordingly
- always use geographical terms in your answers (e.g. compass directions, the scale of the map, grid references)
- if you are requested to use supplementary items to answer questions, ensure these items have your details written on them and are placed inside the front cover of the candidate's answer booklet submitted at the end of the examination

Integrate information from the atlas into your answers across the question paper to achieve better marks. It is obvious to markers when atlas information is used well within the context of an answer and when it is just an add-on with no clear relevance to the question/response.

Never leave early, but use any extra time to read over, add to or amend your answers.

ONLINE

Check out the list of command words and their meanings at www.brightredbooks.net

Marks are given for sketch maps and diagrams that are integral parts of an answer.

ONLINE

Check out the Glossary for this study guide at www.brightredbooks.net

COMMAND WORDS

Command words are verbs or verbal phrases used in questions and tasks to ask learners to demonstrate that they have learned specific skills, knowledge or understanding. Examples are 'describe', 'investigate' and 'how'.

By using past-paper questions, you will become familiar with the command words typically used in Advanced Higher Geography.

THINGS TO DO AND THINK ABOUT

Past papers and marking instructions

The SQA Advanced Higher Geography subject page provides support in preparing and practising for the examination. Use the links at www.brightredbooks.net to access the:

- Advanced Higher Geography Specimen Question Paper
- Advanced Higher Geography Exemplar Question Paper
- Advanced Higher Geography Past Papers – see past papers and marking instructions tab.

These files include the question paper, supplementary items and marking instructions. Download these PDF files and store them on a computer for later use.

The marking instructions published by the SQA provide useful information because they outline the general principles for marking and the detailed marking instructions for each question.

Do take time to read through the marking instructions, bearing in mind that they are designed for markers.

Use them as part of your learning and for revision purposes to check your answers for accuracy.

The 'detailed marking instructions for each question' consists of grids.

Question			General marking principle for this type of question	Max Mark	Specific Marking Instructions for this question
	(c)	(i)	Candidates are not expected to know about nature reserves and so should make use of the map to help suggest reasons	3	RHNR is a coastal location which would provide a rich supply of food for birds. It could act as a 'stop-over point' for migratory species (2). It is an isolated location with no road access and so will provide a suitable environment for wildlife to flourish (1). There are large areas of water for wetland wildlife and shingle ridges which could provide breeding grounds. Good variation/diversity of natural habitats for birds. (2) Any other valid point.

This column outlines the general boundaries for allocating marks. These will vary according to the question.

These are 'possible responses' and not answers. They are guides to allocating marks. Note the final comment: 'Any other valid point'.

MAP INTERPRETATION

PURPOSE

Questions will assess skills in mapping techniques and the ability to use map evidence to support a response. You will use a 1:25 000-scale OS map and other supplementary items.

Refer to SQA Advanced Higher Geography Course Assessment Specification for full details on this question.

Format of the question

The following are typical wordings used in Question 1:

- You should make use of the whole map extract in your response.
- On Supplementary Item B, draw an area of approximately one square kilometre ... e.g. site of a nature reserve
- Draw to scale one suitable site of 100 × 150 metres ... e.g. car park
- Explain the reasons for ...
- Analyse the different impacts of ...
- Annotate Supplementary Item B ...
- Using evidence from across the whole map ...
- Discuss in detail ...
- Suggest possible reasons for ...

The map-interpretation questions are worded in such a way as to allow a degree of freedom in responses, taking into account that:

- responses should be based on evidence from the OS map using place names and grid references
- more than one possible solution can exist when choosing a suitable site (e.g. a nature reserve)
- supporting evidence, reasons for and impacts of, may differ depending on the choices made
- supporting evidence for a choice may be sourced from the atlas or other sources provided
- some responses will include both positive and negative aspects of a choice.

DON'T FORGET

You should make extensive and detailed use of the whole map extract and your atlas in your responses.

Credit is given where a response is clearly backed up by accurate and relevant supporting evidence.

What you already know about Question 1

MAP INTERPRETATION	WHAT YOU FIND OUT ON THE DAY
By practising all the available range of questions during the course and through revision for the examination, I already know that: • Question 1 will o be worth 20 marks o have sub-questions worth two or more marks o use a 1:25 000 scale OS Explorer Series topographical sheet of England and Wales that can be used to assess skills of map interpretation o have typical command words. • The question is about o applying prior knowledge of map-reading and interpretation (e.g. the use of scale, drawing to scale, and interpretation of relief and surface features) o using grid references and references to features symbolised on the map. • Questions in addition to the OS map may also include supplementary items in the form of one or more of the following: o maps or map-based diagrams o photographs o sketches o graphical information or outline drawings o drawings based on photographs o data tables o written text about the area.	On the day of the examination, the specific information revealed will be: • the location of the OS map • the context of the question • the sub-questions and available marks • the command words used • the supplementary items.

contd

OS mapping skills

At Advanced Higher level, it is assumed that you have acquired, from previous learning, a high degree of skill in map-reading and interpretation – for example, measuring distances using the scale, drawing items to scale, recognising the physical and human features symbolised on the map, ability to use four- and six-figure grid references appropriately, understanding of how contours symbolise the height and shape of the landscape, and ability to interpret the effect of relief and surface features.

Advanced Higher OS map interpretation

The 1:25 000 map interpretation at Advanced Higher level uses the same core OS map skills learned previously. These maps, and the expectations at Advanced Higher, bring new challenges.

Useful online sources

SQA past papers include:

- a copy of the OS map, but unless you can print this off to the correct size/scale its use is limited – however, they are worth using electronically on a computer screen
- supplementary items linked to the OS map (e.g. overlays) – the overlay could be printed off and copied onto tracing paper.

The Ordnance Survey provides advice, guides and access to OS maps at OS Maps.

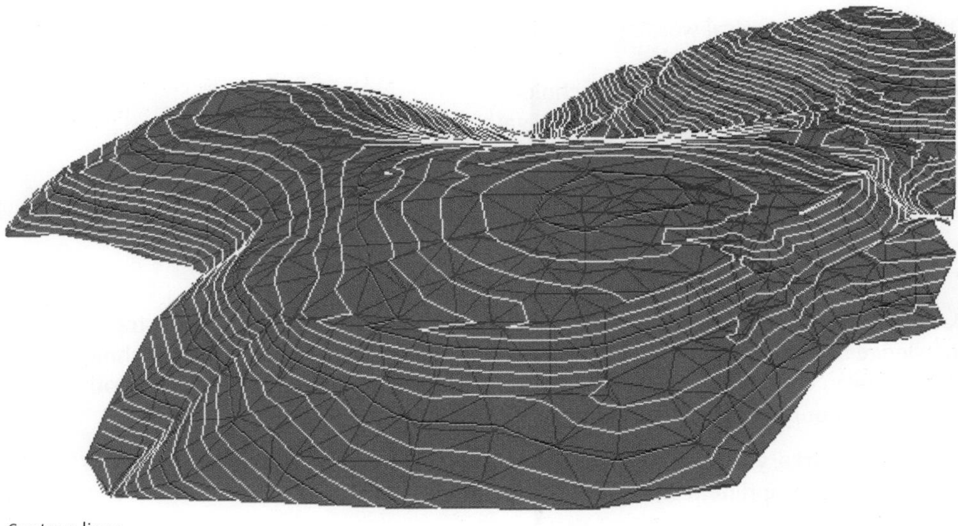

Contour lines.

ONLINE

To revise the mapping skills mentioned here, look at the websites linked from www.brightredbooks.net

ONLINE

Check out these challenges and how to respond to them at www.brightredbooks.net

ONLINE

Find all the relevant links and videos at www.brightredbooks.net

- map symbols
- using grid references
- contour lines.

ONLINE

Head to www.brightredbooks.net for a link to read more about using topographic maps.

ONLINE

Head to www.brightredbooks.net to see some tasks you could use to practise or test yourself.

ONLINE

Head to www.brightredbooks.net to see some OS questions from the 2009–15 past papers you could use to practise or test yourself.

THINGS TO DO AND THINK ABOUT

Refer to the generic advice on pp. 90 and 91 and the following specific points.

The SQA Advanced Higher Geography subject page provides support in preparing and practising for the examination. Use the links on the Digital Zone to access the:

- Advanced Higher Geography Specimen Question Paper
- Advanced Higher Geography past papers.

These files include the question paper, supplementary items and marking instructions. Download these PDF files and store them on a computer for later use.

DATA-GATHERING AND PROCESSING TECHNIQUES AND GEOGRAPHICAL DATA-HANDLING

DATA-GATHERING AND PROCESSING TECHNIQUES

Purpose

Gathering and processing techniques questions will assess knowledge and understanding of data gathering and processing techniques in the context of research/fieldwork and the analysis/evaluation of data obtained as a result of these techniques. Questions may use the supplementary items supplied with the question paper. You will not be asked to carry out calculations or complete tables of data in the question paper. These are assessed at unit level and in the project. The question will sample from the gathering and processing techniques explained within this guide (pp. 8–81).

Refer to the SQA Advanced Higher Geography Course Assessment Specification for full details on this question.

Format of the question

The following are typical wordings used in Question 2:

- Discuss the ways in which ...
- Explain at least three effective techniques ...
- Outline the physical and human data-gathering techniques ...
- Discuss an appropriate sampling technique ...
- Explain factors ...
- On Supplementary Item C, draw an appropriate ...
- Comment on problems ...
- Explain two effective techniques ...

Data-gathering and processing questions are worded to allow you to demonstrate your knowledge and understanding of a range of data-gathering and processing techniques within a given context. Be aware that skills, knowledge and understanding from other parts of the course may be used when answering these questions.

To gain full marks, you have to ensure your answer for the given context refers to:

- the most appropriate technique(s) for the given context
- appropriate methodologies
- issues/problems using a particular technique, if required
- the effectiveness of the technique(s)
- relevant information from an atlas.

Check out the past paper-questions and marking instructions to get an idea of what is expected by markers.

What you already know about Question 2

DATA-GATHERING AND PROCESSING TECHNIQUES	WHAT YOU FIND OUT ON THE DAY

By practising on all the available range of questions during the course and through revision for the examination, I already know that:
• Question 2 will
  o sample from the prescribed list of techniques (pp. 8–37)
  o be worth 10 marks (5 + 5)
  o have sub-questions worth two or more marks
  o have typical command words.
• The question is about demonstrating knowledge and understanding of:
  o data-gathering techniques in the context of research/fieldwork (pp. 8–37)
  o data-processing techniques through the analysis/evaluation of data obtained as a result of using these techniques (pp. 38–81).
• Questions
  o may use the supplementary items supplied with the question paper
  o will not ask me to carry out calculations or complete tables of data in the question paper.
	On the day of the examination, the specific information revealed will be:
	• the data-gathering technique sampled
	• the processing technique sampled
	• the context of the question
	• the sub-questions and available marks
	• the command words used
	• supplementary items for question 2.

GEOGRAPHICAL DATA HANDLING

Purpose

Geographical data-handling questions will assess the interpretation and analysis of a given set of data, including statistical data, to evaluate techniques and their effectiveness in explaining geographical relationships. Questions will use the supplementary items supplied with the question paper.

This question will sample from the statistical, graphical and mapping techniques explained within this guide (pp. 38–81).

Refer to the SQA Advanced Higher Geography Course Assessment Specification for full details on this question.

Format of the question

The following are typical wordings used in Question 3:

- Explain the distribution of ...
- Evaluate the effectiveness of ...
- Evaluate the validity of this null hypothesis ...
- Explain factors that could account for ...
- Account for differences ...
- Discuss the suitability of ...
- Discuss possible reasons for ...

Geographical data-handling questions are worded to allow you to demonstrate your knowledge and understanding of a range of processing techniques within a given context using supplementary items, which might including data tables, maps, graphs and statistical information. Skills, knowledge and understanding from other parts of the course may be used when answering these questions.

To gain full marks, you have to ensure your answer for the given context refers to:

- reasons for the distribution shown on a map
- reasons for using one or more techniques for the given context
- an evaluation of the effectiveness of a technique
- issues/problems using a particular technique(s), if required
- differences resulting from the use of one or more techniques
- relevant information from an atlas.

Check out the past-paper questions and marking instructions to get an idea of what is expected by markers.

What you already know about Question 3

GEOGRAPHICAL DATA-HANDLING	WHAT YOU FIND OUT ON THE DAY

By practising on all the available range of questions during the course and through revision for the examination, I already know that:
• Question 3 will
  o sample from the prescribed list of techniques (pp. 38–53)
  o be worth 20 marks
  o have sub-questions worth two or more marks
  o have typical command words.
• The question is about
  o interpreting and analysing a given set of data, including statistical data
  o evaluation of any techniques used
  o the effectiveness of these techniques in explaining geographical relationships.
• Questions
  o may use the supplementary items supplied with the question paper
  o will not require calculations or the completion of tables of data.
	On the day of the examination, the specific information revealed will be:
	• the statistical technique(s)
	• the context of the question
	• the sub-questions and available marks
	• the command words used
	• supplementary items for Question 3.

THINGS TO DO AND THINK ABOUT

Refer to the generic advice on pp. 90 and 91 and the following specific points.

The SQA Advanced Higher Geography subject page provides support in preparing and practising for the examination. Use the links at www.brightredbooks.net to access the:

- Advanced Higher Geography Specimen Question Paper
- Advanced Higher Geography past papers – see past papers and marking instructions tab.

These files include the question paper, supplementary items and marking instructions. Download these PDF files and store them on a computer for later use.

Make detailed use of your atlas in answering questions.

INDEX